Political Sociology series

William T. Armaline, Davita Silfen Glasberg
& Bandana Purkayastha, *The Human Rights Enterprise:
Political Sociology, State Power, and Social Movements*

Daniel Béland, *What is Social Policy?
Understanding the Welfare State*

Cedric de Leon, *Party & Society:
Reconstructing a Sociology of Democratic Party Politics*

Nina Eliasoph, *The Politics of Volunteering*

Hank Johnston, *States & Social Movements*

Richard Lachmann, *States and Power*

Siniša Malešević, *Nation-States and Nationalisms:
Organization, Ideology and Solidarity*

Andrew J. Perrin, *American Democracy:
From Tocqueville to Town Halls to Twitter*

John Stone & Polly Rizova, *Racial Conflict in Global Society*

Racial Conflict in Global Society

John Stone and Polly Rizova

polity

First published in 2014 by Polity Press

Polity Press
65 Bridge Street
Cambridge CB2 1UR, UK

Polity Press
350 Main Street
Malden, MA 02148, USA

ISBN-13: 978-0-7456-6260-2
ISBN-13: 978-0-7456-6261-9(pb)

A catalogue record for this book is available from the British Library.

Typeset in 11 on 13 pt Sabon by
Servis Filmsetting Ltd, Stockport, Cheshire
Printed and bound in Great Britain by T.J. International Ltd, Padstow, Cornwall

For further information on Polity, visit our website: www.politybooks.com

This book is dedicated to our graduate students in the Sociology Department at Boston University and the Atkinson Graduate School of Management at Willamette University who, because of their diversity, humanity and intelligence, have managed to transcend any trace of global conflict.

Contents

Acknowledgements

While this book is dedicated to our graduate students at Boston University and the Atkinson Graduate School of Management, we would also like to acknowledge our debt to so many friends and colleagues who have shared their ideas and wisdom with us over the years. As we cannot possibly mention them all, we will simply note our appreciation to our fellow editors on the *Encyclopedia of Race, Ethnicity and Nationalism* (Wiley-Blackwell, 2014), Rutledge Dennis, Xiaoshuo Hou and Anthony Smith.

We would also like to thank Jonathan Skerrett at Polity Press for his assistance and encouragement, and Helen Gray for her most helpful editorial suggestions.

John Stone and Polly Rizova
Boston and Portland, 2013

Introduction

In this book, we have attempted to present an analysis of racial conflict as it has taken place historically and against a broad comparative context. Although we are both sociologists by training, this problem area requires an appreciation of other perspectives across the social sciences and historical studies in order to understand the types of debates that have occurred in a highly controversial and complex field. A fundamental premise of our approach is that no single explanatory system can provide the reader with a comprehensive appreciation of the dynamics of racial conflict and that a better strategy is to consider race relations, alongside ethnicity and nationalism, as one of a series of divisions that has been employed to shape the nature of group relations. If any one approach can be isolated to explain the manner in which racial conflict is generated or reduced it is the relative power that one group has over another. It is for this reason, and because of the subtlety of Weber's exploration of power relationships in societies around the world, that we have chosen to adopt a neo-Weberian perspective throughout this volume, following in the tradition of the seminal writings of the great German sociologist of the early twentieth century. Furthermore, it explains why this book fits in well with a series exploring different themes within political sociology.

Weber's writings date mainly from the first two decades of the last century, an era that was very different from today, when Europe was still the home of powerful states dominating vast areas of Africa, the Middle East, South America and Asia. And racial ideas and race relations reflected this overwhelming imbalance in power and influence between individuals and groups that were considered by many to consist of different types of peoples. In some respects, Weber's early ideas retained some of the inherent biases of the age in which he lived and it could be argued that few of his key works focused centrally on matters of race and ethnicity. Nevertheless, the overall framework he developed to explain the emergence of modern industrial society, and its impact on social life, provides easily adaptable concepts that can be applied as readily to racial as to social stratification, and to ethnic and national struggles as much as to class conflict and political divisions. In the early chapters, we will outline some of Weber's struggles with these issues and how race, power and conflict are key themes in the central argument in the book. Ideas about the true significance of 'race' have changed fundamentally over the past century; so too has our understanding of the complexities of power and our assessment of different types of conflict and their impact on group relations.

While Weber, along with Marx, is generally seen as a contributor to the conflict school of sociological theory, there are important differences between the two influential thinkers (Giddens 1971, 1981). It is not that the Weberian approach 'refutes' Marx's emphasis on class conflict so much as develops it in a more complex manner to take into account a range of other factors that influence and drive social conflict and change. Recognizing the importance of ideas, values and culture as critical forces in shaping conflict and social change has particular value in a field where passionate beliefs about racial superiority and inferiority have been endemic. Thus, racial ideas cannot be simply dismissed as largely irrelevant in the struggles between different groups for privilege or justice. In the same way, the power of nationalism to mobilize populations to fight and die for 'their' country, to seek autonomy from dominant groups living in the same political unit or to conquer territories that they believe are historically part of the nation, should not be dismissed as mere financial or economic manipulation, as a crude Marxist interpretation might suggest. Without ignoring the strength of material factors, we argue that ideas, beliefs and values – no matter how misguided or downright bizarre they may appear to outsiders, or with the benefit of hindsight – must also be included in the analysis.

In the first chapter, we look at definitions of race, power and conflict to demonstrate the complexity of these superficially straightforward concepts. Although the idea of 'race' is based on false, pseudo-scientific ideas, it does not mean that racism can be simply dismissed as ignorance and folly. The powerful impact of the 'social construction of reality' – that once individuals and groups start to believe that something is true, it becomes very real in its consequences – must not be overlooked. There is a parallel here between the way that Weber famously discusses the central role of Calvinist belief systems in the development of early capitalist activity at the start of the Industrial Revolution, with the practical power of racism in forging racial conflict. This is followed by a discussion of Weber's emphasis on the boundaries between groups and the importance of 'social closure' – building on an analogy between the tendency for capitalist markets to create monopolies in the economic sphere – as a fundamental cause of the strongly cohesive character of many racial and ethnic groups. The importance of these boundaries, and the various mechanisms that are used to enforce them, are explored in greater detail in chapter 3. Subsequent sections of the first chapter further examine how racist ideas provide legitimacy to systems of racial exploitation and stratification, and then we introduce the theme of globalization that, both in the past and increasingly in modern times, has begun to impact the balance of power between major states and the racial and ethnic groups who live within them.

The argument in chapter 2 explores some of the issues highlighted by the general shifts in power resulting from globalization and recent internal changes within major multi-racial societies. While recognizing that these are matters often associated with 'world system' theorists, a branch of neo-Marxism that stresses the role of economic exploitation between all societies influenced by capitalist trading and manufacturing relationships, the actual outcome of contemporary shifts in the global economy are less one-sided than the empires of previous centuries. This is because economic development and wealth are not simply being drained from the developing world to the more advanced economic states of the developed world, but have come about as a result of an increasing transformation of world production, so that much of the global manufacturing capacity, as well as the service-sector industries, are being outsourced to new locations. Enhanced migration flows, the growth of substantial middle classes in countries like China and India, and the economic strains faced by displaced factory and office workers in North America and Europe, all have serious political and social implications for global power relations.

Two illustrations of such changes can be found in a discussion of the arguments concerning the blurring boundaries between racial and national groups in the United States and Europe. We will consider the provocative arguments put forward by leading thinkers in this area, notably Rogers Brubaker and Eduardo Bonilla-Silva, to consider the degree to which we are entering a 'post-ethnic' or 'post-racial' situation, where shifts in power are fundamentally redrawing the contours of group life. Then we will look in greater detail at the debates surrounding the impact of global capitalism, both historically and in contemporary times, to see how market forces are likely to impact race and ethnic relations. The chapter concludes by exploring the development and changes in patterns of race relations in three critically important societies, China, Brazil and South Africa, to see the extent to which similar shifts in power relations have, over the centuries, helped to shape the emerging forms of group relations on three different continents. The contrasts and similarities with the experience in Europe and North America provide a useful test of the universality, or otherwise, of our general analysis.

The third chapter returns to the central issue of the nature of boundaries and identity in the changing world of the twenty-first century. We start by examining the experience of the United States and the claim that some scholars and political leaders have made that it has a unique history that makes it different from other societies in certain important respects. This concept of 'American exceptionalism' dates back to the foundation of the Republic and received its classic formulation in the writings of

Alexis de Tocqueville in the 1830s. While Tocqueville, a French aristocrat living in the aftermath of the revolution of 1789, was focusing on the democratic political experiment in the early years of the new republic, the question remains about how exceptional the American experience actually is, and whether this applies to the patterns of race and ethnic relations in that country. One answer to this question can be explored by comparing and contrasting the United States with the societies of the European Union as far as race, ethnicity and nationalism is concerned. Our discussion includes the rising salience of Islam and the reaction of both continental powers to increasingly ethnocentric movements and political parties that have been characterized as part of a trend towards Islamophobia. The United States' military intervention in the Muslim-dominated societies of Iraq and Afghanistan, and the increasing number of migrants from the Islamic world currently living in European societies and in the US, has raised the issue of religious (ethnic) conflict to a new level.

Our next chapter looks at the manner in which the increasingly diverse workforces affect the structure and functioning of organizations, both at the national and international levels. In this case we move beyond the more traditional Weberian analysis of modern bureaucratic organizations, characterized by managerial hierarchies and rigid rules specifying appropriate forms of behaviour, to look at the new and experimental forms of organizational design and incentives associated with 'learning organizations'. These new models pay much greater attention to the variability of cultural beliefs and norms found in an increasingly diverse and global employment structure, at both the managerial and workforce levels. Global industries are searching for talent from all over the world in order to compete in a marketplace for labour and consumers that recognizes few state boundaries. But despite these trends, previous patterns of racial and ethnic hierarchy have not completely dissolved as the complex developments in the United States clearly demonstrate. One important explanation for this rests with the continuing significance of social networks when it comes to finding and gaining employment, since these are frequently based on racial, ethnic and national associations. Evidence from the United States, Russia, China and the Middle East reveals how racial and ethnic stratification in employment is perpetuated – classic examples of Weberian 'social closure' – despite the growing diversity associated with globalization.

We then turn our attention, in chapter 5, to the most extreme types of racial conflict. These situations of war, genocide and violence have received surprisingly little attention from sociologists despite their powerful impact on millions of individuals and every society at one historical period or another. After briefly outlining the reasons for this lack of attention in the mainstream sociological tradition, we focus on the Weberian analysis of power yet again, by examining the situation of many indigenous peoples and their struggles for survival when confronted by explorers and settlers from societies possessing more powerful technologies and weapons. The contrasts between the situations in North America and Russia (the Soviet Union), and the reasons for the degrees of decimation of native peoples throughout the world, once again fit in with a Weberian perspective on power.

A further illustration of war and violence brings in the overlapping fields of racial conflict and nationalism. Just as in the case of race and ethnic relations, so in scholarship on nationalism, arguments have centred on the issue of whether nationalism has its roots in deep-seated centuries of tradition, a 'primordial' source of identity and affiliation, or whether most forms of nationalism are socially constructed and can therefore be quite new in their creation. The 'invention of tradition' is a favourite term of the 'modernists' who view nationalism as a recent development in world history despite the claims and fervent beliefs of many contemporary nationalists. As Weber saw it, nationalism is the political expression of racial or ethnic groups who seek to create an independent political unit, a state, to be the exclusive domain of a particular self-defined group. In the modern era, the near impossibility of creating a state that is the sole homeland of a single ethnic group results in the conflict and violence that frequently accompanies extreme nationalist movements. Warfare and genocidal massacres are so often defined in exclusive racial, ethnic and nationalist terms.

The concluding chapter returns to the age-old enigma of how to reconcile the claims of diverse racial and ethnic groups and whether political policies or structures can produce viable solutions to the problem of justice and diversity. Once again, we return to Weber's emphasis on power and its distribution in order to understand the difficulty of achieving reasonable and effective solutions to these questions. While forces at the global level, such as the post-Cold War political realignments and the destabilizing consequences of the 'War on Terror', have altered the climate in which such solutions are being sought, at the state level certain policies have been implemented with varying degrees of success.

We examine the policies described generally under the label of 'affirmative action' that have been pursued for up to a century in India and for shorter periods in the United States and Malaysia, and more recently in societies like Brazil and South Africa, to see the extent to which they provide some answer to rectifying the imbalances in power between different racial and ethnic groups. Finally, we consider two contrasting cases where the outcome of racial and ethnic conflict has not followed the path predicted by conventional wisdom, or indeed by many social scientists. These are the successful transition towards multi-racial democracy in post-apartheid South Africa, a result that appeared highly unlikely before the 1980s; and the destructive collapse of the former state of Yugoslavia into inter-ethnic warfare and massacres, despite the fact that it had previously been viewed as one of the most likely candidates for a peaceful transition into a democratic federation after the collapse of communism. Understanding the subtle changes in power relations and the ways in which a variety of forces operated to produce these contrasting outcomes serves as a further illustration of the insight of the neo-Weberian perspective.

Throughout our book we are well aware that there are other theories and models of social conflict and change that have been used to explore these important issues. Scholars who are more closely associated with a variety of Marxian and neo-Marxian analyses would tend to place a greater stress on the economic factors operating in each situation. So, too, would those writers in the neoclassical economic tradition who also focus on impersonal market forces as a key to understanding why events move in the direction they do. There are many sub-fields that stem from these overall perspectives, whether world systems theories on the one hand or rational choice models on the other, but none of these approaches, in our opinion, provide greater insight into the dynamics of racial and ethnic conflict than ideas derived from the Weberian tradition. There has also, periodically, been a revival of ideas that tend to stress more inherent biological characteristics to account for group formation and affiliation – sociobiology and genomics – which we consider to provide little extra insight into group relations and to have potentially dangerous implications that such differences are generalizable and unalterable. The history of racism should make us very careful when dealing with these types of arguments, just in the same way that Weber chose to dismiss such theories as he found more plausible social and political explanations for group variations. Hopefully, developments in neuroscience – for example, the current excitement about mapping the internal operations of the human brain – will not move in this direction either, and become a twenty-first-century version of phrenology, the nineteenth-century pseudo-science which claimed that examining the bumps on the head could predict personality and other behavioural characteristics.

Other approaches are more closely based on the experiences of a particular society and these tend to focus on the special characteristics of one society and the particular circumstances that gave rise to patterns of racial domination, resistance and change in that unique setting. The great weight of American scholarship and the central theme of slavery in United States history, while hardly exceptional, nevertheless have tended to concentrate attention on factors that may not be equally important in other societies. A recent symposium and critique of the influential writings of Omi and Winant on 'racial formation theory' (*Ethnic and Racial Studies*, June 2013) seems to focus on whether the authors are simply '"evading white racism" and underestimating the persistence of racial structures in the "colorblind", "post-racial" language of a contemporary white frame'. As Rutledge Dennis perceptively remarks, what is needed is a careful analysis of 'how racist systems may be altered and changed' (2013: 988) and to do this requires a broader comparative perspective (see also Michael Banton's comments 'In Defense of Mainstream Sociology' in the same symposium, pp. 1000–4). So, while we will be referring briefly to alternative interpretations of racial conflict throughout the book, the neo-Weberian emphasis on power will be the guiding thread of our analysis.

1

Diversity

Conflicts in the New Millennium

It should be quite clear to any observer of societies in the twenty-first century that major changes in the political, economic and social structure of the modern world are transforming the environment in which all peoples live. This is particularly noticeable in the case of industrialization with the rise of the newly emergent economies in Brazil, Russia, India, China and South Africa (often referred to collectively as the BRICS countries).[1] The shift from the traditional centres of industrial manufacturing, such as the United States, Japan and Europe, towards these other states has produced a corresponding realignment of political strength. Such trends can only be expected to increase over time. In this book, we seek to demonstrate some of the implications that these global changes are likely to produce on the patterns of race relations and, in particular, on the levels of racial conflict around the world. We are starting from the basic premise that race relations are a subset of power relations so that the two forces are intimately connected. Before we can proceed with this analysis it is essential to define what we understand by *race, power* and *conflict*, the three central terms in our approach.

Race, power and conflict

The idea of 'race', a concept that has no scientific basis in fact, raises so many of the crucial elements that we will be discussing

11

throughout the book. Sociologists have long recognized that 'the social construction of reality' (Berger and Luckmann 1966) implies that ideas or knowledge that may have little or no scientific validity can, nonetheless, be devastatingly important in social life. What the political scientist, Donald Horowitz, has acutely captured as 'the figment of pigment' (1971: 244) is yet another variation on W. I. Thomas's famous dictum that 'if men (people) define situations as real they are real in their consequences' (Thomas and Thomas 1928; Merton 1995). In other words, while no serious contemporary student of human biology or genetics would suggest that you can meaningfully divide the world into distinct groups based on visual criteria like the colour of their skin or the shape of their heads or bodies, these ideas were very common in the nineteenth and the first half of the twentieth century. The reason for this lies not in biology but in the differences in the geographical distribution of power and resources which, in turn, superficially suggested a causal connection between certain physical characteristics and so-called 'levels of civilization'. This, of course, was a convenient rationalization for colonialism and the imperial domination by European states, as well as the emerging powers of the United States and Japan, of much of the rest of the world (Go 2011). Thus, the idea of 'race', linked as it was to imperialism and several centuries of racial slavery, came to be used by powerful groups as the justification to exploit those they had been able to conquer and dominate.

Power is a rather different concept, but one that is by no means easy to define. Awareness of the importance of differences in power has not simply been the basis of political sociology but of politics itself from the earliest days of human settlement and the growth of towns. But what exactly is power? One of the most useful basic definitions was provided by Max Weber who argued that power is the ability to make people do what you want, even if it is against their own wishes and interests (Weber 1922). As a starting point this is quite helpful, but there are other dimensions of power that make the concept even more complicated when you start to analyse specific situations. In an influential re-evaluation of these issues, Steven Lukes has pointed to the 'three faces of power' (Lukes 1974, 2005; Swartz 2007) that lead from the brutal imposition of control by physical force and violence – tanks, secret police and other draconian measures associated with authoritarian regimes – to the more subtle processes of selective socialization, persuasion and influence. These can run the gamut from media commercials, religious pronouncements and political ideologies to extreme forms of thought control that include indoctrination and brainwashing. The ultimate type of control, as George Orwell pointed out in his political satire *1984*, is to persuade people that their interests and those of their rulers are one and the same.[2]

Conflict, the third of our key terms, is also much more complex than it is often portrayed. The general association of conflict with violence as seen in warfare, genocide and other forms of severely destructive actions is but one type of conflict activity. Another less violent manifestation of conflict, usually referred to as competition, which can take place in economic, political and social realms, is often a more common form of conflict between different groups. In some cases, as Max Weber's contemporary, German sociologist Georg Simmel, pointed out at the beginning of the twentieth century, such competitive struggles can actually serve to strengthen the long-term stability of the social order by allowing for dissent, innovation, social mobility and the peaceful resolution of group differences under the banner of democratic regimes (Simmel 1908; Coser 1956). This broader conceptualization of conflict is particularly important when considering measures to reduce racial conflict and promote inter-group trust and cooperation. However, even this approach raises a diverse set of issues concerning the desirability, or even feasibility, of maintaining the completely free expression of ideas in an environment recovering from severe forms of racial and ethnic conflict. In other words, what are the limits of free speech in the aftermath of genocidal massacres perpetrated, at least in part, by a relentless barrage of hate speech? The ban on Nazi political parties and the outlawing of anti-Semitic propaganda in post-Second World War Germany, or the prohibition on references to ethnic affiliations like Hutu or Tutsi in post-conflict Rwanda (Straus 2006; Longman 2011; Canellos 2012)), are two such examples of the limits of tolerance towards intolerance.[3]

A neo-Weberian perspective

So, if 'race' is a false idea that has been used historically as a principal explanation for group inequality, and power and conflict are complex concepts that are, nonetheless, valuable to expose the dynamics that underlie group membership and struggle, how can Weber's formulation unite the three elements? Weber's basic analysis of racial and other types of group conflicts starts from an analogy between economic and social processes. In his research on economic history, Weber noted the tendency for economic activities to develop in the direction of monopolies. Gaining control over the supply of particular goods or services would allow a producer to fix prices and eliminate unwanted competition. If we apply this tendency to social life more generally, the advantages of creating groups with distinct boundaries for membership, and therefore fostering a related process of monopolizing the benefits for insiders rather than outsiders, become obvious. Such a perspective helps us to understand the similarities between groups whose identities can be based on a whole series of different characteristics. These may include ethnicity, nationalism, religion, language and class (gender and sexual orientation might also be added to the list although they have certain distinctive properties of their own), and such groupings answer the puzzle of why some conflicts are based primarily on race and others on religion, language or ethnicity.

Weber's explanation for this was that the choice of boundary markers is a result of historical circumstances, almost chance encounters between groups who differ from one another because they happen to speak a particular language, adhere to a specific religion or have a different physical appearance, but who were also very unequal in terms of their control of resources and power. Once the initial contacts have taken place, the more powerful will tend to strengthen group markers and erect boundaries to maintain and increase their control over the less powerful. This helps to explain why in one situation, Belgium, for example, language has become a crucial symbol of group membership; while in another, Northern Ireland, 'religion' (nationalism) has been vital; and in yet another, the United States, 'race' (skin colour) has been the most powerful boundary marker. Of course, just as these situations emerge out of differential power relations so they will change over the years as groups struggle to alter their position in the power hierarchy or, indeed, strive to eliminate such differences altogether.

While this formulation offers a broad sketch of the often rational underpinnings of group membership, persistence and survival, the reality is much more complicated. Weber's approach to sociology in general also emphasized the role of the individual's understanding and interpretation of social life (*verstehen*), thereby bringing variables like culture and belief systems, non-material factors, into a more rounded and nuanced analysis. Actors do not always think or behave in an entirely rational manner, or at least their 'rationality' is imbued by cultural values, traditions and emotions that cannot be reduced to a simple and universal political (or economic) formula. This is particularly true in the area of race relations where a complex amalgam of conflicting values, identities and other factors may be crucial to understanding what is actually going on.

Race, ethnicity and nationalism

Weber's ideas about race, ethnicity and nationalism evolved over his lifetime. Some of his earliest writings in the 1890s were based on empirical studies of rural life in eastern Germany. These involved comparisons between ethnic Germans and ethnic Poles, both as farmers and as farm labourers. In these early studies, Weber displayed a thoroughgoing German nationalism in which he castigated the Junkers, the landed aristocracy, for using cheap Polish labour that undercut and systematically displaced German farm workers from the great estates of the eastern parts of the country. At this time, Weber had not totally rejected the influential notions in the late nineteenth and early twentieth centuries of inherent racial differences, as his references to 'Slavic adaptability' implied, but he was much too careful a scholar to pursue this line of reasoning without substantial evidence to support it. Time and again, he found concrete historical and social causes to explain observable differences in the economic behaviour and social status of the Polish and German populations, which made the idea of inherent group characteristics redundant. His growing rejection of racial theorizing was not based on a conviction that no such differences could exist, and even in his later writings he always regarded the question, at least in principle, as an open one. What was crucial for Weber was the weight of evidence that the work habits of Germans and Poles were a product of historical circumstances and environmental conditions rather than permanent biological or cultural attributes. As a result, references to such variables increasingly faded from Weber's subsequent writings on these issues.

There are two other major themes in Weber's work that illustrate this consistent rejection of racial 'explanations' of historical change and national character. In contemporary debates about the factors claiming to explain the decline of the Roman Empire, Weber attacked the notion that 'barbarian' blood among the leadership groups could in any manner account for the collapse of this great civilization. Such a hypothesis simply did not fit the facts. At the height of its power and prestige, the Roman Empire acquired many of its most brilliant leaders from the ethnic periphery of its vast territories, and there is no evidence that it was external rather than Roman cultural influences that accompanied the social and political disintegration of the empire.[4] Explanations had to be found in other, less simplistic causes. In writing about another of the great historical civilizations, that of the Chinese, Weber addressed the same basic issue from a different angle. He considered the question of outsiders' stereotypes of the Chinese 'character' and demonstrated how these were often mutually contradictory or that certain types of behaviour could be interpreted as typical of most groups under similar circumstances. Once again, Weber's commitment to value-neutral methods to explore and test hypotheses, considered to be eminently plausible by many contemporary scholars, led him to reject racial explanations of social and political events.[5]

Weber's mature position on race and ethnicity, and the stratification based on these criteria, thus represents a significant and vital shift from the emphasis of his turn-of-the-century writings on rural life in Eastern Prussia. This is further illustrated by his analysis of the Indian caste system and the situation of post-diaspora Jews in Western societies. Manasse provides a balanced assessment, pointing to the crucial change in the type of question that Weber considered to be important in these later studies. The confusion between race and culture was resolved and 'instead of asking which innate qualities distinguish one Indian caste from another, he raised the question why the solution of the racial problem in India differed so greatly from the solution in analogous situations, such as that in England after the Norman Conquest' (1947: 207). A similar change of focus could be detected in his attempt to understand the factors inhibiting the assimilation of Jews in the diaspora by their host societies. Turning away from any allegedly hereditary characteristics of the Jews as a minority group, he asked, 'What historical and sociological experiences shaped those attitudes that caused the segregation of Jews from their neighbours?' (ibid.).

In both cases, Weber's interest in the historical development of the caste system or in the remarkable persistence of the Jews as a distinct minority – or 'pariah group' to use his more controversial terminology – caused him to focus on the interaction between economics, religion and ethnicity. Economic monopolization provided much of the rationale for the creation of these particular social structures, religion served as a potent source of legitimation, and racial or ethnic characteristics acted as convenient types of group markers. He saw caste as originating in racial conflict, with the dominant, light-skinned conquerors forcing the darker-skinned, indigenous populations out of those occupations that carried social prestige. Understanding the religious doctrine of karma and the taboos against intermarriage and commensality provided, as in his argument about the unique contribution of ascetic Protestantism to the birth of modern capitalism, vital clues to the resilience of the caste system in India. A similar appreciation of the special characteristics of traditional Judaism, such as the emphasis on strict dietary laws, also played an important part in explaining why the Jewish people had preserved their distinct communities in a largely Gentile world.[6]

It can be seen from these illustrations that the scope of Weber's vision was impressive but the specific contributions that have remained crucial for the field may be considered under the following broad headings: (a) the insight of his basic definitions; (b) the process of group closure and boundary maintenance; (c) the role of racist and other ethnocentric ideas, and the importance of legitimacy; and (d) the centrality of power and domination. When it comes to definitions Weber was as interested in ethnicity as in race. His evident frustration with the elusive quality of ethnicity is well captured by many of his statements on the subject in *Economy and Society*. Nevertheless, he did not abandon the concept and proceeded with great care to try to isolate its essential character. As a result, he produced a formulation that has been adopted, in most of its basic elements, by many subsequent scholars of the subject. Weber defined ethnic groups as 'human groups (other than kinship groups) which cherish a belief in their common origins of such a kind that it provides a basis for the creation of a community' (Runciman 1978: 364). In this definition, he isolates the fundamental characteristics of the phenomenon that centre on a set of beliefs and not on any objective features of group membership such as shared language, religion, and especially biological traits associated with the everyday understanding of race. It is this sense of common ancestry that is vital, but the identification with shared origins often turns out to be largely, if not totally, fictitious.[7]

The elusive quality of ethnicity stems from the minimal core on which ethnic groups are based and accounts for the variety of other elements that are found among the many examples of individual ethnic groups. Weber is adamant that the difference between ethnic groups and kinship groups lies precisely on the question of 'presumed identity' (Roth and Wittich 1968: 389). Ethnic membership per se does not necessarily result in ethnic group formation but only provides the resources that may, under the right circumstances, be mobilized into a group by appropriate political action. This leads on to a discussion of nationalism, another closely related concept in the analysis of race and ethnicity. Weber's view of nationalism was a political extension of the ethnic community that arose as its members and leadership sought to create a unique political structure by establishing an independent state (Smith 1992b: 62–3). However, as Anthony Smith has noted, he did not provide an historical account of the rise of nationalism, but he did, nevertheless, seek to discuss the important relationship between ethnicity and nationalism, which has been a key feature of much subsequent scholarship.

Group closure and boundary maintenance

Apart from providing these basic definitions of race, ethnicity and nationalism, Weber's discussion of what he termed 'social closure' is another particularly helpful contribution to our understanding of the origin and dynamics of ethnic and racial groups, which we outlined earlier. Not all social scientists, however, have agreed that boundary-closing mechanisms are entirely a random product of historical circumstances. Writers such as Murphy (1988) proposed a hierarchy of closure mechanisms rather than the almost random process of group demarcation suggested by Weber. The theme of social closure has become an important element in the neo-Weberian literature; while it has been developed with particular focus on social stratification, it is of equal if not greater relevance to ethnic and racial stratification.

Frank Parkin's (1979) trenchant critique of Marxism, along with subsequent studies by Murphy and Brubaker, has demonstrated how 'the mechanisms of closure provide a key to understanding the formation of status groups and social classes engaged in the struggle over the distribution of rewards and opportunities' (Manza 1992: 276). Although much of this debate has been concerned with aspects of class analysis, many of the examples have in fact been drawn from situations of deep racial and ethnic conflict. This has exposed the limitations of the sociology of stratification that has ignored or downplayed these critical ethnic and racial divisions and it is true of gender as well. As a result, modern strati-fication theory has steadily regained a wider vision that typifies the approach found in Weber's writings on these issues rather than being preoccupied by the more restricted view of the mechanisms associated with economic classes found in industrial societies.

Concepts of closure, and the related question of group bounda-ries, can be seen as a central preoccupation of many scholars studying ethnicity in modern society. Michael Hechter's work, for example, has ranged across a spectrum of issues, from concerns with the phenomenon of internal colonialism as an explanation for the regionalist movements in the Celtic Fringe of Great Britain (Hechter 1975; Stone and Hechter 1979) to rational choice analy-ses of ethnic conflict (Hechter 1986, 1987). Both approaches, while very different in the levels of analysis and explanation, have some connection to questions of social closure, but his theoretical discussion of the principles of group solidarity clearly lies explic-itly within the debates over types and forms of social closure. In social anthropology, the seminal writings of Fredrik Barth on boundaries, and the subsequent focus of scholars such as Wallman and Okamura, represent variations on a similar theme (Barth 1969; Okamura 1981; Wallman 1986). Brubaker's (1992) study on *Citizenship and Nationhood in France and Germany* reveals yet another illustration of the manner in which Weber's emphasis on the centrality of social closure continued to appear in influ-ential studies of societal diversity. As Brubaker notes: 'In global perspective, citizenship is a powerful instrument of social closure, shielding prosperous states from the migrant poor. Citizenship is also an instrument of closure within states. Every state establishes a conceptual, legal and ideological boundary between citizens and foreigners.' (1992: x)

Although it is not generally attributed to the Weberian legacy for the sociology of race and ethnic relations, as it is usually associated more with work such as Simmel's classic essay on 'The Stranger', Park and Stonequist's writings on 'the marginal man', or Du Bois' analysis of 'double consciousness' (Du Bois 1903; Simmel 1908; Park 1928/1950; Stonequist 1937), the body of lit-erature devoted to 'merchant (or middleman) minorities' can also be linked to Weber's interest in what he called 'pariah groups'. Such merchant minorities were a common feature of colonial societies where the imperial power would encourage the migration of groups that were of a different racial, ethnic or religious background to act as intermediaries between the colonizers and the colonized. Sometimes they became traders and merchants; in other cases they would be recruited as troops or police officers, whose loyalties to the colonial rulers ensured some privileges in the system but also generated great resentment from the indigenous populations. Once decolonization took place those intermediary groups were frequently the early targets of riots, looting and expulsion as seen in the aftermath of independence in Indonesia, Malaysia and Uganda (Horowitz 1985). The parallels between the experiences of colonial merchant minorities, and the violent persecution of Jews and Armenians in European societies, point to the similar structural position of marginality facing all of them. It also demonstrates how changing power relations in the wider society can have devastating consequences for those caught in between the past and current dominant political powers in society.

Although it is true, as Gary Abraham has stressed, that Weber's concern with such minority groups was only a side issue to his major research interests, his analysis should not be dismissed, as Abraham implies, as simply a repetition of 'contemporary stereotypes' (1992: 293). His interpretation of the position of such groups in society contains much insight that is derived from seeing the phenomenon in a broad comparative context. Thus, the ideal type may be based on the situation of European Jewry, but the characteristic features of a merchant minority can be found in a variety of groups residing in many different societies during various historical epochs. Among such groups, tendencies towards monopolization, albeit forced on the group by outside discriminatory pressures, can be developed with the assistance of ethnic markers or religious sanctions that are then used to limit access to group membership. Such status differentiation merges into caste-like structures, according to Weber, only when rooted in ethnic divisions. Thus:

The caste is actually the normal 'societal' form in which ethnic communities which believe in blood relationships and forbid intermarriage and social intercourse with outsiders live alongside one another. This is true of the 'pariah' peoples which have emerged from time to time in all parts of the world – communities which have acquired special occupational traditions of an artisan or other kind, which cultivate a belief in their common ethnic origin, and which now live in a 'diaspora', rigorously avoiding all personal intercourse other than that which is unavoidable, in a legally precarious position, but tolerated on the grounds of their economic indispensability and often even privileged, and interspersed among political communities ... The Jews are the most striking historical example. (Runciman 1978: 50)

Later scholars have argued about the balance of characteristics that constitute the core features of such groups and particularly about the factors in the wider societies, and among the groups themselves, that account for the origin and persistence of the phenomenon. Others have criticized Weber for the apparently pejorative connotations of the term 'pariah group', but substitution of politically more correct terminology such as 'middlemen' or 'merchant minorities' should not disguise the fact that these particularly vulnerable ethnic groups display many of the sociological characteristics found in Weber's original analysis of the subject.

Racism and legitimacy

Two of the most distinctive features of Weber's sociological perspective were his concern for understanding the meaning that individual actors attributed to their behaviour and the related importance that they invariably attached to the search for legitimacy in relation to such action. In *The Protestant Ethic and the Spirit of Capitalism* (1904–5), Weber isolated a special set of ideas that he argued were especially crucial in explaining why modern rational capitalism took off in a particular social setting during a specific historical period. Several sociologists and historians of race and ethnic relations have also speculated on the parallel role of ideologies and belief systems – in this case, those associated with racism – in contributing towards an explanation of the dynamics and persistence of particular forms of racial and ethnic stratification. John Rex, for example, who was one leading sociologist to explicitly identify with a Weberian perspective, incorporated the presence and special character of 'deterministic belief systems' in his attempt to define a 'race relations situation' (Rex 1970, 1980). However, other scholars, particularly those inclined towards a Marxist interpretation, have tended to dismiss racial ideas as epiphenomena that are largely insignificant reflections of a particular mode of production, but much of this is based on confusion concerning the social impact of false ideas. It is certainly the case that ideas of biological races have been discredited on scientific grounds – as we stressed earlier, notions of 'pure races' are wholly fictitious – but it is not the case that such beliefs are sociologically irrelevant. For Weber, it did not matter whether Calvinist notions of predestination had any validity; what counted was that people believed this to be the case and that this had real, if unanticipated, consequences for human action.

While it is true that there is no absolute link between prejudiced beliefs and discriminatory action (Merton 1949), to dismiss such ideas as irrelevant is unjustified. Thus, Rex focused on the debates over slavery and pointed to the importance that Weber attached to 'the question of the role of religious and other ideological factors in shaping socio-economic systems' (Rex 1980: 125). Although Weber's stress on the affinity between Calvinism and rational capitalism might imply an incompatibility between slavery and capitalism, the situation was in reality much more complex than this. Rex uses Weber's basic approach to develop a broad sociological portrait of colonialism and post-colonial societies that revealed how 'slavery was one means of achieving ends which may also be achieved through a variety of alternative forms of unfree labour' (ibid.: 130). Where then does racism enter the picture? On this question, Rex makes the interesting claim, following both Tocqueville and Weber, that racist ideas tend to be particularly salient in circumstances where legal sanctions no longer support racial inequality. Under these conditions, the social order has to 'depend upon the inculcation in the minds of both exploiters and exploited of a belief in the superiority of the exploiter and the inferiority of the exploited' (ibid.: 131). In this way, as Rex continued to argue, 'the doctrine of equality of economic opportunity and that of racial superiority and inferiority complement one another. Racism serves to bridge the gap between theory and practice' (ibid.).

Such a position not only suggests that racial ideas are far from irrelevant, but highlights the circumstances where they may be critically important. It also raises the second major preoccupation of Weber's sociology of domination: the question of legitimacy. For, as Weber noted: '[There is] the generally observable need of any power, or even of any advantage of life, to justify itself . . . He who is most favoured feels the never ceasing need to look upon his position as in some way "legitimate", upon his advantage as "deserved", and other's disadvantage as being brought about by the latter's "fault" (Weber 1922/1968: 953; also quoted in Wrong 1979: 104). Slavery, apartheid and other forms of racial oppression were generally associated with elaborate ideological justifications, but it may well be the case that racist ideas are particularly important when such rigid status systems are being questioned and are under attack from egalitarian social philosophies. Those following in the Weberian tradition would have little doubt that such ideas should be taken seriously and analysed as part of the causal chain that brings about systems of racial hierarchy, helps them to endure, and also leads to their eventual demise.

Power and domination

Many, although by no means all, interpreters of Weber's political sociology have noted the element of naked power that lies ominously below the surface of his discussion of legitimacy and authority. As Frank Parkin comments, 'inside the velvet glove is always the iron fist . . . the terminology of violence, coercion and force is as natural to Weber's sociology as the terminology of moral integration is to Durkheim's' (1982: 71). Weber himself is quite explicit about the matter and in *Economy and Society* declares:

> Domination in the most general sense is one of the most important elements of social action. Of course, not every form of social action reveals a structure of dominance. But in most of the varieties of social action domination plays a considerable role, even where it is not obvious at first sight ... Without exception every sphere of social action is profoundly influenced by structures of dominance. (Weber 1922/1968: 941)

This insight is particularly relevant for the study of race and ethnic relations, and it is no accident that an important survey of the state of global race relations written by Philip Mason during the late 1960s, and based on research monographs from all five continents, should have been given the simple title of *Patterns of Dominance* (Mason 1970). Mason was neither a sociologist nor someone particularly influenced by Weber's writings, but the choice was characteristically Weberian in its stress on structures of power conceived in a broad manner. Weber's preoccupation with power has a special resonance for studies of race and ethnic relations, even though these were not his primary focus of interest. By breaking down the components of power and stressing the analytically distinct concept of 'status group', Weber opened up a means of understanding the special sociological nature of ethnic group formation that had so long troubled those trying to impose a largely materialist perspective on ethnic loyalty, racial identity and national affiliation. The example of the poor whites in the Southern states of America is frequently cited by Weber as a dynamic illustration of the interplay between low economic class and high ethnic status, which has such important repercussions for race relations. While explaining the lack of class conflict between the plantation owners and the non-slave-owning whites, he noted that: '"the poor white trash" was much more hostile to the Negroes than the planters, who, because of their situation, were often swayed by patriarchal feelings' (Runciman 1978: 58). In this way, he draws a distinction between what Pierre van den

Berghe (1965, 1978) was to characterize as the 'competitive' and 'paternalistic' ideal types of race relations.

Van den Berghe's work comparing race relations in South Africa in the early era of apartheid (1948–90), and the patterns of relationships between blacks and whites that characterized the American South prior to the 1960s Civil Rights movement, also noted the shift towards greater openly expressed hostility once the stability of the racial order was being challenged. This, of course, did not mark the end of a system of 'inter-racial harmony' that many of the white segregationists wished to believe, but rather opposition to the injustice of racial exploitation and the violent reactions used to suppress it. The superficial acceptance of the earlier period masked a situation of overwhelming domination in which opposition that did occur from time to time was ruthlessly suppressed. As a movement of more sustained demands for change, combined with greater support from outside forces, gathered momentum, the facade of inter-racial goodwill and acceptance dissolved and hostility on both sides of the colour line could not be denied. This was as true for the American South as it was for apartheid South Africa.

The influential discussion of 'class, status and party' in *Economy and Society* also points to the special spheres in which market conditions prevail and those areas in which they do not, anticipating some of the limitations of rational choice-based theories of race relations (Banton 1983; Hechter 1987; and, for a summary critique, see Avruch 2012: 106–13). Thus, Weber notes that 'when the fate of a group of men is not determined by their chances of using goods or labour in the market (as in the case of slaves), that group is not in the technical sense a "class" but a "status group"' (Runciman 1978: 45). This does not mean that status groups are unrelated to the economic structure of society, but it does imply that their special dynamics are not wholly driven by the mode of production, by the distribution of wealth in society, or by a set of preferences originating, in any meaningful way, at the individual level. Race and ethnic relations have been defined by one later social scientist, Herbert Blumer, as a 'sense of group position' (Lal 1990: 49–64), which is very close to the preoccupation with social worth, prestige and styles of life that are the hallmarks of status groups in general and ethnic groups in particular, as found in the Weberian conceptualization. Whereas it would be wrong to deny the direct economic costs and benefits associated with ethnic and racial group membership (and exclusion), a purely materialist explanation totally fails to capture the complex reality of some of the most fundamental bases of individual identity and social life.

Despite the theoretical primacy of power in Weberian sociology and its practical relevance for studies of race and ethnic relations, these two aspects of social relationships are not always closely associated. Of the major sociological perspectives on race and ethnic relations, the writings found within the plural-society tradition are perhaps the most explicitly Weberian in their emphasis. These start from Furnivall's classic description of a 'plural society' (1948: 304–11), formulated in relation to Burma and Indonesia under colonial rule. The plural society was one consisting of separate ethnic and racial groups living in distinct social spheres and cultural universes, where group interaction was confined to the impersonal relationships of the marketplace and where the whole society is held together by the political power of the dominant (colonial) rulers. Such a model has many of the ingredients of Weber's approach, including the recognition of the social reality of discrete ethnic and racial boundaries, and the fundamental significance of power in underpinning group relationships. Its subsequent development by M. G. Smith and Leo Kuper (Kuper and Smith 1969) revealed even more parallels. Thus, Smith's focus on what he called the 'differential incorporation of minority groups' is not unlike the mechanisms of closure that we discussed earlier. What is noteworthy is that much of this literature refers to the societies of the Caribbean and sub-Saharan Africa, reflecting the degree to which these concepts have broad cross-cultural relevance.

The more we consider the manner in which racial and ethnic groups are the product of differential power relationships in societies around the world, the greater the value of a global perspective becomes apparent. This was true of Weber's many studies, particularly but by no means exclusively in his writings on religion and economics, where he contrasted the influence of Western Calvinism in forging the 'spirit of capitalism' with the socio-economic impact of religions in India and China, and under ancient Judaism, but becomes increasingly relevant to a world connected more closely by the forces of globalization. We will now explore some of the consequences of these more recent trends and assess the extent to which they conform to our more general framework.

Globalization

One of the effects of the end of the Cold War was to open up large sectors of the world economy to capitalist penetration. While this process was an acceleration of trends that were clearly apparent in the later decades of the twentieth century, and indeed had been operating in one form or another for centuries, it did pose the question of the impact that a freer exchange of capital and goods would have on the future patterns of international migration. That in turn has been one of the major forces generating the racial and ethnic diversity of the leading industrial and commercial regions of the world. Exactly how this would work out at the dawn of the twenty-first century was made more intriguing by other changes, for example, those induced by technological trends that allowed the integration of production and consumption in ways, and on a scale, that had not been possible previously. 'Outsourcing' is one such development that was intimately linked to global capitalism, but had an entirely unconventional impact on human migration. The capitalists and managers of the multinational corporations could enjoy the benefits of cheaper labour, as indeed could the consumers, without having to negotiate immigration rules and regulations set up, at least in part, to preserve the economic protection of blue- and white-collar citizens in wealthier societies.

However, despite these interesting innovations, much of the almost universal trend towards a global capitalist mode of production had entirely predictable repercussions. Migration to the United States, the European Union, Japan and other advanced economies continued to expand both legally and, often even more significantly, in illegal forms. This resulted in conventional types of exploitation, conflict, integration and assimilation, depending on the society of origin and the racial and ethnic structure and history of the society of destination. On occasions these flows moved against the traditional patterns, myths and ideologies concerning migration. Thus, both Ireland and Italy (O'Dowd 2005), whose experiences for most of the nineteenth and twentieth centuries were steeped in a history of population loss and struggles against intolerance overseas, found themselves in the reverse situation. They had become (albeit temporarily as the Great Recession of 2008 was to demonstrate) affluent economies, acting as magnets for the less wealthy migrants of Eastern and South-eastern Europe, as well as the much poorer states of North Africa and the sub-Saharan region. The result was a move by most members and institutions of the host society towards establishing boundaries and defining the new migrants as stigmatized 'outsiders'.[8]

Such a volte-face could also be seen in the 'society of immigrants' where many commentators demonstrated a similar form of historical amnesia, declaring that the composition of more recent flows to the United States was structurally different from that of the proportionately more significant migration waves of the 1880–1920 period. Thus Samuel Huntington, refining still further his *Clash of Civilizations* thesis, argued that because the majority of the Mexican/Latino migrants came from, or through, a society sharing a land border with the United States, it places them in an altogether different situation from the previous waves of transatlantic migrants at the turn of the twentieth century (Huntington 1996). In addition to the territorial connection, which, it is argued, enhances a form of transnational contact and identity, there is also the history of inter-state warfare and land dispossession that Huntington suggested might well stimulate 'revanchist sentiments' (Huntington 2004: 221–56). Thus, in one of the interesting quirks of history, 'the results of American expansion in the nineteenth century could be threatened and possibly reversed by Mexican demographic expansion in the twenty-first century' (1996: 206). The very success of military conquest in one era may generate a demographic Trojan horse, resulting in what an earlier commentator characterized as an 'Alien Nation' (Brimelow 1995).

The close proximity of the United States and Mexico may have something to do with the ratio of legal to illegal migrants when there are economic incentives for migrants to make the risky and expensive journey across the border. Between 2001 and 2004, the number of legal permanent residents entering the United States fell from 578,000 to 455,000, but the number of illegal immigrants increased from 549,000 to 562,000 (Passel and Suro 2005). The number of border apprehensions, those migrants detained and subsequently deported, fell by 61 per cent between 2005 and 2010, from 1,189,000 to 463,000. The impact of the Great Recession, starting in 2008 and resulting in a rapid decline in employment opportunities for migrant workers, can be clearly shown in this precipitous drop in the number of people attempting to come to the United States. Tightening border security appears not to have much impact and the failure of the American administrations to sanction those who employ illegal workers reflects the divided attitude of a government, many of whose supporters desire access to cheap labour while seeking to maintain a firm image concerning national security in the wake of the 9/11 terrorist attacks.

Similar trends can be seen in Europe, where an expanded Union is both trying to absorb the new member-states economically and to preserve the 'Fortress Europe' strategy towards the peripheral societies on its borders. Just as the Rio Grande is viewed by many anxious Americans as the Southern frontier of the United States subject to penetration by poverty-stricken Latinos and also potentially by 'terrorists', so the Spanish enclaves, like Melilla and Ceuta in Morocco, have witnessed the death of African immigrants rushing the border posts in a vain attempt to get into Europe (Woolls 2005). Little has changed since van Amersfoort stressed the limits of governmental control and the failure of strategies in most European states to discourage the employment of illegal immigrants.

The (control) measures have in any case not been successful in the sense that there is still a steady amount of illegal work in all West

European countries, employing illegal residents and thereby attracting new immigrants. It should be realized that this 'shadow labour market' is not only for immigrants neither is it only part of the shadowy side of the economy in seasonal agricultural labour, summer work in small family hotels or in 'entertainment houses'. It is also part of the official economy, in international airports, top hotels and the fashionable sportswear industry. (van Amersfoort 1996: 255)

In many respects, then, the United States and Europe resemble each other in the manner that they attract migrants from a variety of different sources and are either unwilling or unable to place effective exclusionary barriers to prevent their entry and employment.[9] Even a society that has often been characterized as ethnically homogeneous, like Japan, has been described by at least one serious scholar as 'multi-ethnic' (Lie 2001). Clearly, those aspects of globalization that have stimulated labour movement and, in some cases, produced a more fluid transnational lifestyle are not confined to the highly educated global elites (Nishida 2008; Jain 2011). Similar lifestyles can also be seen among diasporic communities and in growing numbers of conventional migrants, assisted by inexpensive air transport and multiple forms of communication. Furthermore, the impact of these developments on the next generation raises many important issues (Levitt and Waters 2002; Portes and Rumbaut 2006), an interesting example of which is the return migration of well-educated Americans of Indian background to their parents' homeland to set up new businesses and to work in the high-technology sectors of the economy (Jain 2013).

One explanation for the apparent impotence of states to control these forces can be seen in the relative strength of state and non-state actors in the current global capitalist system. When major corporations like Walmart, Microsoft, Intel, Apple, General Electric, Exxon-Mobil and Hewlett-Packard, to take some prominent American multinationals, have market capitalizations in excess of the GNP of many developed and developing countries (e.g., Spain, Kuwait, Argentina, Poland and Thailand), there are serious implications of such inequalities of wealth and power for both inter-state and intra-state relations. These in turn will have potentially important repercussions on racial and ethnic groups that are differentially affected by the globalizing impact on wealth distribution and its control in the hands of non-democratic actors. As one analyst has concluded, concentrated corporate influence is unprecedented in the post-Cold War period so that 'no socialist economy has ever had the command and control capacities of the American corporation' (Mitchell 2001). Furthermore, there is consistent evidence that the market policies associated with the current phase of globalization have dramatically increased inequality *within* most developed states.[10]

Bringing Weber back in

What we have argued in this chapter is the centrality of power in understanding the global experience of racial and ethnic conflict over the past few centuries. While race relations were not the major theme of most of Max Weber's writings,[11] there is enough insight in his basic approach to society to incorporate these fundamental divisions into his overarching framework. The interaction between power, group formation and conflict can be seen to operate in both historical and comparative contexts to provide a plausible explanation for the origin of racial hierarchies in many societies and to reveal the forces contributing to changes over time. We live in a global era of fundamental change, where power is no longer concentrated in certain regions of the world that happen to be dominated by individuals and groups with similar cultures and appearances. If past experience is any guide, these changes will have fundamental repercussions for the balance of power between different states and this will undoubtedly be accompanied by changing perceptions and behaviour rooted in traditional racial hierarchies. The more perceptive social scientists in the past understood the dynamic nature of these relationships and anticipated the changes that would almost certainly follow in the decades to come. However, the prognosis is not entirely favourable since the very forces that resulted in Eurocentric domination in the past need not necessarily lead to a more universalistic outcome in the future. Should one group of relatively homogeneous people gain disproportionate power over other groups, then it is entirely to be expected that new patterns of racial hierarchy could then replace the current situation. However distasteful that may be to those who prefer justice over tyranny, and equality over exploitation, it must be recognized that past ideas of 'progress' have so often proven to be naive. History has a habit of repeating itself.

2

Power

The Changing Geo-politics of Race

In the second chapter, the argument is developed regarding the central role of power in determining the evolution and perpetuation of systems of racial and ethnic stratification, by looking more closely at certain theories that emphasize different aspects of this approach. The global extension of classical Marxism found in world systems theories offers one such perspective and while it has a considerable degree of plausibility, given the levels of economic exploitation associated with colonialism and slavery, we feel it has limitations in explaining current developments in the changing world power system. The complex pluralism of Weber's modifications to Marxism, integrating the role of political forces in addition to ideologies and belief systems is, in our opinion, a superior model for understanding the linkages between changing power structures and race and ethnic relations. Subsequently, an alternative economic analysis will be examined, which turns Marxism on its head and argues that market forces, in an approach typical of many neo-conservative thinkers, can in fact dissolve the barriers and divisions of race, ethnicity and nationalism in a far more effective manner than political movements and interventions. Once again, we doubt the plausibility that Adam Smith's 'invisible hand' alone – the inspiration for this type of thinking – will be any more effective in breaking down racial and ethnic barriers than the revolutions advocated by neo-Marxist thinkers.

Then we consider two influential and contrasting assessments of the direction of race and ethnicity in the twenty-first century, starting with the arguments of Rogers Brubaker concerning the diminishing significance of ethnicity and nationalism, particularly with respect to Central Europe in the post-Soviet era. This is followed by the critique of 'post-racialism' as applied to the United States, exemplified by the writings of Eduardo Bonilla-Silva, in the wake of Barack Obama's successful campaign to become the first African American to be elected president in 2008 and his subsequent re-election four years later. In each case, exaggerating the significance or insignificance of group boundaries has its limitations. The chapter concludes by exploring changes in the patterns of race and ethnicity in China, Brazil and South Africa. These three societies have very different historical experiences of racial and ethnic conflicts but represent dynamic and changing societies that can be usefully compared to the evolving situations in Europe and North America.

The analysis of racial and ethnic conflict, and its attempted resolution, draws on a broad and eclectic field of disciplinary knowledge. For sociologists, the idea that conflict is endemic in human society has been recognized since the beginning of the discipline. The issue is less the removal of conflict per se, something, as we mentioned in the previous chapter, that Simmel – Weber's contemporary and friend – and many others regarded as a futile quest, but more the challenge of how to channel the conflicting forces found in all societies in a less destructive and, hopefully, more positive direction. Such a search applies as much to the tensions within groups as it does to the conflicts between them. And this is another important illustration of where race and ethnic theories intersect with the analysis of nationalism (Conversi 2002), which will be explored in further detail in chapter 5.

Materialism and racial conflicts

The world systems approach is one that emerged in the 1970s from earlier analyses inspired by Marx's interpretation of nineteenth-century capitalism as part of a larger historical process. This evolutionary perspective was a common feature of much nineteenth-century social thought, no matter whether the writers were critics, like Marx and Engels, or supporters, like Herbert Spencer, of the current state of society, and saw social change moving through a series of stages towards a more advanced and better condition. Both branches of this 'progress' theory, whether revolutionary or evolutionary, were based on interpretations of the European experience of social change – and as a consequence were heavily biased towards Eurocentric assumptions – which were then applied to the rest of the world. Viewing the 'world system' as an essentially interconnected whole, for at least the past five centuries, is a perspective that has had much appeal, particularly to scholars on the left (Wallerstein 1974–2011; Chase-Dunn 1991) but also to the advocates of global free markets on the political right. One of the major criticisms of the Marxist perspective in the social sciences, but one that is equally applicable to market theorists, is that its excessive focus on economic variables virtually excludes any other motivating forces in human history. This is particularly damaging when it comes to the fields of race relations and nationalism where passionately held beliefs and values – no matter how misguided or fictitious they may be – often lead to outcomes that are impossible to explain in terms of economic self-interest alone. The idea of 'false consciousness', the failure of oppressed classes to understand the true source of their exploitation, a concept that was invented by Marx and Engels to account for these glaring anomalies, hardly provides a convincing explanation of what is taking place.[1] When writing in 1870, Marx did note both national and racial divisions among the proletariat, 'a working class divided into two hostile camps', about which he elaborated in the following terms:

> The ordinary English worker hates the Irish worker as a competitor who lowers his standard of living. In relation to the Irish worker he feels himself a member of the *ruling nation* and so turns himself into a tool of the aristocrats and capitalists of his country against Ireland, thus strengthening their domination *over himself*. He cherishes religious, social and national prejudice against the Irish worker. His attitude towards him is much the same as that of the 'poor whites' to

the 'negroes' in the former slave states of the United States of America. The Irishman pays him back with interest in his own money. He sees in the English worker at once the accomplice and the stupid tool of the *English rule in Ireland*. (Levin and Stone 1985: 9)

Such antagonism between English and Irish workers was carefully nurtured and artificially intensified by the ruling classes, using every means at their disposal. These included 'the press, the pulpit, and the comic papers'. In this way the English bourgeoisie maintained its power by a deliberate strategy of divide and rule. Nevertheless, in Marx and Engels' opinion, such tactics could not succeed indefinitely. History, however, would prove their timescale to be hopelessly wrong. Because of their overarching model of inevitable social change, they failed to see the strength and resilience of attachments to nation and race. This would be revealed time and time again, whether in the failure of the international workers' movements to stop the outbreak of the First World War – proletarians on both sides of the conflict rushing into the trenches to die for King (or Kaiser) and country, completely forgetting any sense of workers' solidarity. Or in the notorious slogan of the South African Communist Party during the 1922 'Rand Revolt' (Stone 1973: 50–2), which proclaimed: 'Workers of the World Unite and Fight for a White South Africa!' Because their model assumed that revolution could only take place after the maturity of the capitalist phase of a country's development, Marx and Engels were completely dismissive of such movements as Pan-Slavism, and therefore the nations of Eastern Europe, but also of Indian society, viewing nineteenth-century British imperial rule as a means to dissolve 'these small, semi-barbarian, semi-civilized communities' and even went so far as to describe China as 'a living fossil' (Levin and Stone 1985: 4).

Such rampant Western ethnocentrism – paradoxically in line with certain of the Social Darwinist currents of their time and contrary to the attitudes of such anti-Marxian figures like Herbert Spencer who, while praising entrepreneurial capitalism, abhorred imperialism – paved the way for a complete underestimation of the power of racism and nationalism in the longer term. Had Marx and Engels lived into the early twentieth century they would have been forced to reassess these factors and probably would have shifted rather closer to Max Weber's view that granted the independent causal role of beliefs and cultural values a rather more serious consideration.

Later writers in the Marxist tradition, such as Gramsci and Fanon, also grappled with similar glaring weaknesses in a largely materialist perspective and went on to provide a stronger focus on *hegemony* and the power of ideas to seriously modify the influence of materialist forces. What thinkers on the left and their opponents, who emphasized the long-term benefits of free markets and capitalism, shared in common was a belief in the power of generalized economic factors to shape most aspects of social relations, and this included race and ethnic relations and the forces of nationalism. While Karl Marx and Herbert Spencer face each other in their respective graves at Highgate Cemetery in north London – one of the enduring ironies of the Victorian era – the debate between socialism and capitalism has continued to rage for more than a century after their deaths. The key issue, as far as we are concerned, is whether either system has any significant impact on racial conflict. Let us now turn to some more recent debates that explore this question.

Market forces and race relations

Since the new millennium or, perhaps more precisely, the events of September 11, 2001, and all the related developments flowing from, or in reaction to, this first attack on American soil since Pearl Harbor sixty years before, the analysis of race relations has been in a state of flux. In the United States, the Civil Rights movement of the 1960s has run its course, displaying undeniable progress in several arenas but also a stubborn persistence of much basic racial inequality. What Massey and Denton (1993) aptly termed *American Apartheid* in the 1990s remains as one of the critical realities of life in the United States during the first decades of the twenty-first century – persistent racial segregation (Massey

2007). If an Englishman's home is his castle, for the American where one lives is the pathway to the American Dream. This is because of the fact that, in so many different ways, residence reflects access to the type of educational options available, and these in turn control other crucial opportunities and life chances. The June 2007 Supreme Court ruling that further restricted the use of race in school integration plans – in what many observers view as a mixture of cynicism and Alice-in-Wonderland logic, following Chief Justice Roberts' conclusion that 'the best way to stop discrimination on the basis of race is to stop discriminating on the basis of race' – represents a possible retreat from redistributive policies before any semblance of widespread racial equality has been secured. This combination of historical amnesia and blindness to social reality may well represent a new judicial retreat from Reconstruction that might stop dead, if not reverse, much of the critical progress towards greater racial justice achieved in America since the 1960s.

However, these developments are hardly surprising given the other forces gathering momentum in American society since the attacks on the Twin Towers in Manhattan and the Pentagon near Washington in 2001. Increasing *racial* inequality can be seen as part and parcel of a wider package that has witnessed the erosion of *social* equality in a society driven by the demands of market economics completely disengaged from the fetters of social obligation and regulation. *The Wealth of Nations* has become divorced from *The Theory of Moral Sentiments* in a manner that would have surprised and shocked Adam Smith. Furthermore, the paradox that the free movement of capital is the cornerstone of the global capitalist economy, while the free movement of labour is not, lies at the heart of the conservative dilemma. What is fundamental to 'unfettered' market economics, however, is an increasing trend towards greater inequality and a rolling back of many decades of attempts by the state to act as a mediator and moderating force between entrepreneurial laissez-faire and social justice. This is as true in China as it is in the United States, and, for a period during and immediately after the 1990s, market solutions trumped state limitations in many parts of the world. However, signs have begun to emerge in Russia and Latin America, to take two major examples, of the pendulum starting to swing back to a more balanced position along the continuum between capitalist and socialist economics (Hou 2011, 2013).

This economic backdrop acts as an indispensable context against which to assess the redirection of global ethnic and race relations. It is true that in theory, and sometimes in practice, certain pressures within a market-driven enterprise are largely colour-blind and tend to break down categorical distinctions, but other forces have the opposite impact (Massey 2007). 'Opportunity hoarding', to use the revealing term coined by Tilly (1998) and developed by Shapiro (2004) – rather than the more opaque jargon of social and human capital or network analyses – provides a huge advantage in tipping the playing field in favour of the established participants in the game.[2] It is like a transatlantic boat race in which two yachts start in opposite ports and the one sails with the prevailing winds while the other sails against them. The distance is the same but the outcome is virtually certain, even if the yachts and the crews are identical at the outset. So much for stressing 'merit' when one is blind to the fundamental injustice of the comparison. The increasing economic inequality of both the United States and global society is likely to have repercussions for the progress, or lack of it, found among different racial and ethnic groups. Of course, this may not always lead to a similar impact on *all* racial and ethnic groups, or *every* member of such categories, but the probability is that it will enhance the pre-existing inequalities unless there is some special mitigating factor – like regional concentration or occupational specialization – that may sometimes offset or reduce the inertia of privilege.

To group, or not to group?

Two further developments in contemporary thinking about race, ethnicity and nationalism should also be evaluated in a critical manner. These may be encapsulated in the arguments of two sociologists, Rogers Brubaker (2004, 2013) and Eduardo Bonilla-

Silva (1997, 2006, 2012), derived from very different bodies of literature and research – ethnicity/nationalism in Eastern Europe and race relations in the United States – which arrive at interesting, but contrasting, conclusions. As the seemingly paradoxical titles of their two key books might imply – *Ethnicity without Groups* (2004) and *Racism without Racists* (2006) – these are arguments that suggest a radical deconstruction of the assumptions underpinning much of both areas of scholarship. Brubaker's essays make the claim that ethnic conflict is a catch-all term that encompasses far too much to have any analytical power. Ethnic or national groups do not have the cohesiveness that the leaders of these movements seek to promote, while the conflicts that are labelled 'ethnic' ignore the fact that passionate nationalists are usually a small minority of 'the group' they claim to represent and that much conflict that is falsely categorized as 'ethnic' is often the result of tensions generated by individual, family, class and other factors.

Although there is considerable validity in Brubaker's central claim – that a significant amount of the scholarship on ethnic conflict does indeed focus on those who foment such conflicts rather than on those who ignore or oppose them (2004: 19–20) – the basic thesis does seem to be a clever, but somewhat contrived, way of throwing out the racial or ethnic baby with the conflict bath water. This becomes clearer if we substitute 'organizations' or 'political parties' for 'ethnic groups'. Are we then suggesting that all members working in these organizations or parties necessarily think alike or act in the same manner? Recognizing the diverse motives and beliefs of the membership of groups, however, does not invalidate the structural reality of so many outcomes and certainly does not demand a reductionist approach towards social dynamics. We have had more than enough of this type of analysis over the past twenty years from simplistic rational choice models and the imperialistic claims of sociobiology to the current fad of neuroscience (Stone 1985, 2004; Coulter and Sharrock 2007).

Bonilla-Silva's argument works in the opposite direction. His assessment of American race relations suggests that the apparent move away from state-sanctioned, racial discrimination in the post-Civil Rights era is a myth, or more precisely an adroit repositioning of those forces seeking to preserve the racial boundaries in the United States. By turning the claims of non-racialism against those seeking to implement policies designed to create greater racial justice, policies that are de facto segregationist can hide behind the fig leaf of universalism. The conservative counter-attack against affirmative action, school desegregation, open housing and fair employment is based on a denial of the legitimacy of monitoring, planning or acting with any recognition of racial difference. Thus the Blackmun doctrine, derived from the Supreme Court's 1977 ruling in the *Regents of the University of California* v. *Bakke* case, declaring that 'in order to get beyond race we need first to take race into account', is replaced by a refusal to countenance any consideration of race in public policy. As a result, an absolutist, non-racialism is espoused by some conservatives, which almost guarantees that existing racial inequalities will be preserved indefinitely.

These two approaches to recent developments in the studies of nationalism, ethnic affiliation and racism point to the new types of changes that are taking place in different parts of an increasingly interconnected global society. It is important to understand that not all conflicts should be seen as being based on national or ethnic divisions, despite their labels, just as it is crucial to recognize that long-standing racial boundaries may well be preserved or re-created in a political environment that claims to be actively trying to consign them to the dustbin of history.

Post-racialism: myths and reality

As we stressed in chapter 1, it is generally accepted that 'race' is a social construct, an idea – in this case a scientifically erroneous one – that is in the minds of men and women, whose enormous variability from one society to another, and in different historical periods, demonstrates that it has little intrinsic importance. Nevertheless, the impact of such beliefs can result in a powerful legacy of cultural tradition and social solidarity. While the United States has made substantial progress since the 1960s on the political front with the proliferation of African Americans in high-profile political positions such as Secretary of State, governors and mayors of major states and cities, and the historic election of Barack Obama as president in 2008 (as well as his subsequent re-election in 2012), none of this should divert attention from the continuing significance of racial disadvantage for so much of the black population in the United States. The work of William Julius Wilson (1987) has stressed the need to remember the plight of the 'truly disadvantaged' in the inner cities of America, the indirect and corrosive influence of economic restructuring on the life of the new urban poor (1996), and the fact that such a reality is intimately entwined with persistent poverty (2009). As a result, a disproportionate number of African Americans are still struggling to emerge from generations of oppression and economic disadvantage, which makes talking about a 'post-racial' America premature (Bobo 2011).

A parallel situation can be seen in post-apartheid South Africa, where a revolution in political equality has not been matched with commensurate changes in the distribution of income and wealth. Studies have revealed that despite the growth of a significant African middle class, for the majority of South Africa's people little improvement has taken place in the two decades since the historical transition from white minority rule. In November 2012, President Jacob Zuma commented on the newly released South African Census data for 2011 that showed that the average white South African still earned more than six times the income of black South Africans (Associated Press in *Boston Globe*, 1 November 2012). As the president concluded: 'These figures tell us that at the bottom of the rung is the black majority who continue to be confronted by deep poverty, unemployment, and inequalities, despite the progress that we have made since 1994.' While some improvements had occurred in relation to basic services such as access to clean water, electricity and garbage removal, and more South African families owned televisions than refrigerators, and cell phones rather than electric or gas stoves, nevertheless, the average annual income for a black household was a mere $7,500 in 2011 compared to $45,600 for white households.

The racial disadvantage in the United States was also exacerbated by the impact of the Great Recession, starting in 2008,
which was fuelled by the speculation in the housing sector. This
dramatic collapse in house values seems to have eroded many
of the earlier gains in minority homeownership of the previous
decade that appeared to be important evidence of the narrowing
of the racial disparities along this influential dimension. By 2004,
African-American homeownership had almost reached 50 per
cent, compared to the non-Hispanic white figure of around 75 per
cent. Toxic mortgages, however, disproportionately affected black
and other minority new homebuyers, so that by 2010 the gap
between white and minority homeownership had widened again
and the black–white differential had returned to more than 25 per
cent, a reversion to the racial patterns of homeownership existing
before the bubble burst. (NPR/US Census 2011).

A century and a half since the era of slavery, the impact of
racial divisions lives on, as seen in the continuing discrepancies
in the income and wealth statistics that regularly demonstrate the
deprived status of so many African Americans (Shapiro 2004).
Drive through the heart of any major, or for that matter minor,
American city; examine the student populations of so many of the
worst American public schools or the enrolments in colleges and
universities; or simply consider the statistics describing the inmates
of the American penal system,[3] and the reality of the continuing significance of race is hard to deny. Perhaps a most striking
illustration of the pervasive and insidious nature of racism in the
contemporary United States was the March 2007 vote by the
Cherokee Indians to exclude the Black Freedmen – African slaves
who became a part of the Cherokee nation by the Treaty of 1866 –
and deny these historical co-victims the right to join in the benefits
of tribal economic regeneration.[4] One group of victims seems to
have exhibited little hesitation in victimizing another.

To focus on the North American case is but part of the problem.
However, because of its high ideals – crafted by the slave-owning
proponents of 'democracy' for a relatively small group of white,
property-owning males in the new republic – the United States
has been at the centre of a storm of ethical debates about who

should be granted full membership, and who should be excluded, from the land of the free. The problematic nature of this debate can be seen in the decision of so many black slaves to join the British colonial forces in the 1770s and fight against the advocates of 'life, liberty and the pursuit of happiness', based on a rational calculation that London was more likely to end the 'peculiar institution' than the slave-owning 'democrats' in Philadelphia (Schama 2006). This is not to glamorize the motives of the British who, no sooner had they lost the fight in North America, went on to pillage Africa, Asia and any other parts of the exploitable globe as they scrambled to 'civilize' the rest of humanity. Just as the American dilemma survived to plague the descendants of black and white Americans, so the irony was to come full circle when, in the aftermath of the Second World War, the British employed an 'internal colonialism' analogy – that colonies were colonies no matter whether they were located in the homeland or overseas – to try to defend the persistence of their empire against the anti-imperialist arguments of their former Soviet and American allies (Kirk-Greene 1979). This was a clear reflection of the changed political reality of the post-war years, with the United States and the Soviet Union emerging as the two new superpowers at the start of the Cold War, and the decline of the role of European colonial powers as major economic and military players. In all these cases, it is possible to link the changing power relations with the associated ideologies that were used to justify, or attack, forms of racial and ethnic domination and exploitation that were becoming increasingly contested after 1945.

In other contexts: China

Nevertheless, it would be quite wrong to conclude that racism is in any way confined to the Anglo-American world. The evolution of rather different types of racial hierarchy and group processes can be seen in Asia, Latin America and Africa. In the Chinese case, a whole range of cultural and largely indigenous forces appear to have given rise to a sense of racial identity and hierarchy that had little or nothing to do with Western patterns and culture (Dikötter 1997, 2003). This interpretation of the power of Chinese domestic forces in producing an ethnocentric and independently created form of racism parallels Robert Bellah's classic analysis in *Tokugawa Religion: The Cultural Roots of Modern Japan* (1957), which argued that it was an indigenous blend of Buddhism, Confucianism and Shintoism that underpinned the country's post-Second World War industrial renaissance, rather than the impact of Western contact.

China's notion of a 'yellow race' rested not only on traditional colour symbolism, but even more on the struggles for power among the reformers of the late nineteenth and early twentieth centuries, who reconfigured the traditional emphasis on lineage and family, and synthesized culture, nation and race into their own form of nationalism. Racial discourse in Republican China, particularly following the fall of the Qing Empire in 1911, led to the 'construction of imagined boundaries based on blood' (Dikötter 2003: 129).

As Dikötter insists, 'far from being a "derivative discourse" of a more "authentic" form of "white racism", narratives of blood and descent in China had an internal cohesion which was based on the active reconfiguration of indigenous modes of representation. Lineage discourse was perhaps one of the most prominent elements in the construction of symbolic boundaries between racially defined groups of people' (ibid.: 126). In other words, the Chinese leadership modified traditional folk notions linked to patrilineal descent into the creation of group boundaries, not only between Han, Manchu, Mongols and Tibetans, but also between the 'yellow races' and 'racialized others', whether whites or 'darker races'.

These racial frames of references persisted into the communist era and could be found in popular culture, scientific circles and government publications, despite the universalistic message of Maoist-Marxist ideology and the hostility towards so much that was seen as Western imperialist traditions. Even the radical transition to a rampant form of export capitalism under Deng Xiaoping's leadership after the death of Mao, and the consequent opening up to the West, does not appear to have made much difference to these basic notions. As Dikötter observes, a sense of being Chinese,

> whether in Taiwan, Singapore or mainland China – is primarily defined as a matter of blood and descent: one does not become Chinese like one becomes Swiss or Dutch, since cultural integration (language) or political adoption (passport) are both excluded. Racial discourse, of course, has undergone numerous permutations, reorientations and re-articulations since the end of the nineteenth century. Its flexibility and variability is part of its enduring appeal, as it constantly adapts to different political and social contexts, from racial ideology of an economically successful city-state like Singapore to the eugenics policies of the communist party in mainland China. ([1997] 2003: 133)

The author recognizes the other sources of Chinese identity but argues that 'notions of culture, ethnicity and race have consistently been conflated throughout the twentieth century in efforts to portray cultural features as secondary to an imagined biological specificity' (ibid.). It seems hardly surprising that as China has grown to be the second largest economy in the world, edging out its offshore rival Japan in 2010, perceptions of Chinese communities throughout the rest of the world by other national, ethnic and racial groups have begun to recognize this change in the geo-political balance of power. This is a radical shift from the previously stereotypical views of the Chinese held by many Europeans and North Americans (Keevak 2011). As a result of this change in the relative power balance, the Chinese have an increasing sense of self-confidence while non-Chinese have a growing respect, if not fear, of this new political reality.

Within China itself, the relationship between the dominant Han majority and the relatively small, but in absolute terms highly significant, non-Han minorities remains an unresolved issue. Earlier studies pointed to the contradictions in ethnic policies under previous regimes (Dreyer 1976; Connor 1984) and these tensions have remained during the radical transitions that have transformed contemporary Chinese society (Hou and Stone 2008). Whether we focus on the Han–Hui relationships, the latter being followers of

Islam (Zang 2007), or on the position of the Uighurs, in this case a visibly distinct Muslim minority (Kaltman 2007), similar conflicts remain. Given the overwhelming dominance of the Han Chinese, who comprise more than 90 per cent of the current population of 1.3 billion, it is hardly surprising that ethnic relations are not perceived by many in China as a particularly salient issue. More attention is generally given to the inequalities between the affluent cities and the poor living in the countryside, or problems of corruption among members of the party elites. Nevertheless, because of the gigantic population size of the country, minorities that are relatively small by China's demographic calculus make up more than 100 million people, greater than the population of all but a few major states in other regions of the world.

Two studies based on research conducted between 2001 and 2005 display many of the complexities found in Han–Muslim relationships. While Zang's (2007) investigation focused on Han–Hui relationships, Kaltman's ethnography examined the dynamics of Han–Uighur interaction, particularly in four geographically dispersed locations: Beijing, Shanghai, Urumqui and Shenzhen. In all these sites the Uighur constituted small minorities, living in ethnic enclaves, and even in the capital of Xinjiang, Urumqui, Uighurs made up only 13 per cent of the population in their historic homeland where Islam has its strongest foothold. Han–Uighur comparisons revealed mutual stereotypes, with the majority population perceiving the minority as 'lazy', uninterested in economic development and with a penchant for getting involved in crime. In return many Uighur viewed Han as biased against them and prejudiced against their religious beliefs (Kaltman 2007: 79, 107). However, Kaltman noted clear class differences in Uighur perceptions of the Han, a point that is a central theme in Zang's analysis, despite group pressure against learning Mandarin and the risk of being referred to contemptuously as a 'Chinese Uighur'. It was among the second-generation Uighur migrants in Beijing, where friendship patterns and attitudes towards dating showed distinct trends away from communal solidarity, that a wider appreciation of the benefits of a fluent command of Mandarin, as a means of surmounting the obstacles to social mobility, could be seen.

However, in most of the other enclaves the Uighur seem to have rejected the goals of the more powerful Han-controlled state, posing a nationalist dilemma because the only path to modernity appears to lie in adopting the language and customs of the dominant Han society.

In Zang's study, the emphasis is on Han–Hui relationships in a single urban setting, the city of Lanzhou, and explores several key dimensions of everyday life: neighbourhood interactions, friendship patterns and social networks, various aspects of mate selection and spousal choice, and household structures. The central question is whether high levels of ethnic consciousness can be compatible with integration into the mainstream of contemporary Chinese urban society. The findings suggested both large inter-group variations in social status – the Hui being generally more traditional and the Han more modern – but also some significant intra-group variations in status. This second point is particularly crucial to Zang's basic argument that it is social status, rather than ethnicity, that determines group attitudes and behaviour. Furthermore, once the controls for status are introduced into the multivariate analysis of his survey data, the 'ethnic effect' is virtually wiped out (Zang 2007: 37; Hou and Stone 2008: 814). Thus, the stereotypical assumption that adherence to Islam might impose a distinct type of interaction on all believers does not appear to be the case. Differences occasionally emerge but these are often in the opposite direction from those that many outside observers, and even group members, might anticipate. In Zang's words, 'Ironically, the existing portrayal of the Hui as a densely connected community is true only as it refers to higher status, modern Hui . . . If one argues that the Han are a "lonely crowd", so are the Hui' (2007: 84). At some stages in the analysis, Zang suggests that the Hui elite are actually 'more modern than the Han' (ibid.: 114), thus reinforcing the constantly repeated claim that 'Han–Hui difference is mainly based on ethnic inequality in status attainment' (ibid.: 108).

The difficulty for the Chinese political leadership is how to manage the spectacular economic growth in these multi-ethnic regions and cities without generating reactive ethnic resistance.

As a subsequent study of this issue, focusing on the social impact of these market forces on ethnic minorities in Xinjiang and Tibet, concludes:

> For a Chinese state seeking a complete remedy for ethnic problems through economic growth, both market-driven integration and forced assimilation would be futile. Ethnic diversity will not disappear, and ethnic relations will become even more complex and interdependent under the current conditions of economic and social change. If not dealt with appropriately, increasing social exclusion will continue to occur in China's periphery, especially in Xinjiang and Tibet. This would be truly detrimental to China's goal of building a 'harmonious society' and ensuring sustainable development in its periphery. (Zhu and Blachford 2012: 733)

The problems encountered by China as far as ethnic tensions are concerned have also affected many other South East Asian societies. In some cases, such as Malaysia, Indonesia, Thailand and Burma, countries have their own very complex blends of groups and conflicts. However, it is Japan, East Asia's other great industrial powerhouse that is often seen in much the same light as China, as an overwhelmingly homogeneous society as far as racial and ethnic divisions are concerned. But, once again, a closer look at the actual situation suggests that this too may be a greatly oversimplified assessment. As John Lie has argued in *Multi-ethnic Japan* (2001), even this society defies the mono-ethnic ideology that has been at the core of national identity. A range of minority groups, including the indigenous Ainu and Burakumin, together with Chinese, Koreans and Okinawans, suggests a much more diverse and heterogeneous reality. Then there are increasing numbers of immigrant workers from all over the world – Thais, Malaysians, Filipinos, Pakistanis and Iranians, to mention just a few – expanding the range of diversity in a manner not unlike the flows found in Europe, the United States and other federations and states that view themselves much more as 'immigrant societies' (Lie 2001: 14–21). While Japan and Germany have often been compared as strongly ethno-national states (Brubaker 1992) both have had to shift their policies, if not their cultural beliefs, as a result of globalization and wider geo-political trends. They also share a return of co-ethnics to their societies: ethnic Germans from Eastern Europe and ethnic Japanese from Latin American countries like Brazil and Peru. Such migrants are undoubtedly affected by their years of minority status in cultures far removed from their societies of origin.

The Japanese case has been well summarized by Lie: 'The myth of mono-ethnic Japan is fundamentally a post-World War II construct. The recent vintage of mono-ethnic ideology does not prevent the imagined present from transforming the misty past in its image. Nationalist historiography and the nationalist imagination impose a vision of Japan that has been mono-ethnic from the beginning to the present' (2001: 141). Thus, the Japanese are faced with their own dilemma: a reluctance to welcome immigrants from other East Asian countries at a time of declining birth rates and the continuing ageing of the population. Non-ethnic Japanese residents stood at 2.2 million in 2010, approximately 1.7 per cent of the total population, and these figures comprised some 650,000 Koreans – a legacy of the Japanese occupation of the Korean peninsula from 1905 to 1945 – and smaller numbers of Chinese, Filipinos, Vietnamese and Indonesians (Hockstader 2010). One response to the problem of a declining population has been an unsuccessful attempt to encourage Japanese couples to have more children; another has been the free flow of Brazilians and Peruvians of Japanese ancestry to return to the country, reaching around 500,000 since the 1990s. However, neither trend is sufficient to reverse the demographic decline and it will be interesting to see if, in the future, these pressures will lead to a change in policy and corresponding attitudes of the Japanese towards large-scale immigration. If so, this will be a parallel development to that predicted by Richard Alba (2009) when he argued that the 'blurring of the colour line' in the United States might be a predictable result of demographic changes brought on to a considerable degree by large-scale immigration.

Another form of distorted racial and ethnic perception can be found in the very different societies of Central and Latin America, of which Brazil is a good example.

In other contexts: Brazil

As Edward Telles has argued in *Race in Another America* (2004), Brazil can be considered to be plagued by a powerful tradition of racial distinctions although the dynamics of race relations follow a different logic from that underlying the pattern found in the United States. Despite the ideology of 'racial democracy', the absence of rigid colour barriers in families and other intimate social relationships, formulated in its classical manner by Gilberto Freyre in *The Masters and the Slaves* (1933), few would seriously deny that Brazilian society is permeated by considerations of colour consciousness. The fundamental difference is, in some cruel paradox, that dark-skinned individuals under the rules of the Brazilian system, can, so to speak, 'change their race', while, conforming to the pressures of the one-drop rule, blacks in America cannot. Individualism, which is a prized trait in the United States and embedded in a philosophy of social mobility, nonetheless has the greatest difficulty trying to breach the colour line. The very fluidity of the Brazilian system makes it a more subtle and complex problem to solve,[5] just as declaring 'mission accomplished' in a conventional military campaign is an altogether different proposition from trying to 'win' a war on terrorism.

The value of comparing different racial systems has long been appreciated; the temptation to view one situation from the perspective and assumptions of another is a persistent danger. As Telles notes, the dominant academic interpretations of Brazilian race relations seem to oscillate between two models, the one suggesting that there are virtually no differences between the United States and its southern hemisphere neighbour as far as the outcomes are concerned: in both states a social hierarchy persists in which whites remain at the top of the economic pile and blacks stay at the bottom. The alternative scenario stresses that the differences are in fact profound and persistent, as witnessed by the ideology of miscegenation and social relations that celebrate close and intimate inter-racial bonds. In an attempt to resolve these contradictory interpretations, Telles proposes that a more nuanced analysis is called for so as to reveal the complex combinations of similarities and differences between the two societies. Clearly, interpersonal relations appear to be far more fluid in the Brazilian case, a blurred boundary along the range of a colour continuum that distinguishes between blacks, browns and whites, but also recognizes a kaleidoscope of variations within and between these categories. If many Brazilian immigrants in the United States attempt to 'dance around the one-drop rule', as Catarina Fritz has argued (Fritz 2011), in their society of origin it is a positive car-nival of colours that stands in the way of rigid social segregation. That said, when evaluating the economic winners and losers of the system, the pattern in either hemisphere has a similar complexion.

Some of the explanation can be found in disaggregating the sta-tistics from different parts of the two continental-sized states. Just as historians and social scientists recognize how a diverse legacy has framed the enduring structures of segregation and integra-tion in the North, South and West of the United States, so in the 'other America' regional differences in population mixes, wealth and immigrant histories have influenced the subsequent patterns of inter-group relationships in a crucial manner. In the same way that few scholars of North America would fail to appreciate the diverse legacies of Mississippi and Massachusetts, so, too, it is equally important to understand the contrasts between Sao Paulo, Minas Gerais or Pernambuco. It is also essential to remember major demographic differences between the two societies and the fact that Brazilians with African ancestry represent a far greater ratio of the total population (46 per cent in 2000; around 50 per cent by 2008) compared to the relatively small size of African Americans (13 per cent at the same times). However, slavery per-sisted in Brazil for several decades longer than it lasted in America, which should caution us from drawing overly simple conclusions about the precise meaning of the 'racial democracy' promulgated by Freyre and his followers.

Telles's interesting attempt to resolve the problem rests on a distinction between what he calls vertical and horizontal relations. On the former, whites are at the economic and political summit of society and blacks are at the bottom. Thus, the two societies mirror each other as far as racial stratification is concerned. On the latter, in relation to close personal bonds and mixing at the most intimate levels, the two systems could not be further apart. Such a formulation is difficult for the observer from North America to understand since the logic of US group relations does not accept such a 'contradiction'. In virtually all instances where minorities have mingled, and particularly in the wake of large-scale and persistent intermarriage, the inevitable result has been the rapid assimilation of the minority group into the mainstream core.

Thus, according to Milton Gordon's (1964) classic formulation of American assimilation theory, intermarriage is seen as the final and irreversible dimension in the overall process. The concern of some rabbis and community leaders about the high levels of intermarriage prevalent among American Jews – some seeing intermarriage as an even greater threat to group survival than crude anti-Semitism – is a reflection of a similar assumption about the *inevitable* outcome of such relationships. The persistently low levels of black–white intermarriage – some 0.7 per cent in 1970, three years after the *Loving* v. *Virginia* landmark Supreme Court ruling overturning previous legal barriers to inter-racial marriage in many states, to around 3.9 per cent in 2008 (Pew Research Center Report [US Census American Community Survey] 2008; see also Herman and Campbell 2012), and the higher rates found between many young Asian Americans (particularly women) and whites – are seen as accurate predictors of radically different future trajectories for the two groups. Thus, to return to the 'horizontal' openness of the Brazilian relationships across the colour line, such a pattern simply does not translate for most North American analysts, whose society of study maintains a stubborn hierarchy of whites at the top and blacks at the bottom, with very restricted social intercourse. Even the burgeoning middle-class, suburban black communities in cities like Atlanta and Washington, DC, and poorer white communities in Boston, Buffalo, Philadelphia or Chicago, are also still highly segregated.[6] This is, of course, not a uniquely American phenomenon as Carl Nightingale demonstrates in his book on global patterns of urban segregation (Nightingale 2012), but it is particularly powerful in the North American context as residence is the key to so many other building blocks of the American Dream. Good-quality public education, neighbourhood safety, local services and even access to healthy food are closely correlated with where one lives in the United States.

The overlaps and contrasts between the racial patterns in Brazil and the United States raise vital questions about how the two systems, which had considerable similarities at certain stages of their historical development, went on to generate quite different mechanisms of racial stratification and interpersonal relationships. The Brazilian–US connections, apart from the sizeable migration of Brazilians to certain parts of the United States, are made quite clear in the realm of social policy. Nowhere can the contrasting impact of the two systems of race relations be better seen than in the adoption of affirmative action policies used as an attempt to rectify the colour biases in university admissions (the more general case of affirmative action will be discussed in greater detail in chapter 6). While the battles in the American case are frequently about which clearly defined groups – blacks, Native Americans, immigrants and women – truly merit such reparatory actions and whether social class should be factored into the formula used, in Brazil the key issue is determining who belongs to which groups. One result of the sheer complexity of the Brazilian gradations of colour is that it is actually possible for members of the same (genetic) family, in some cases identical twins, to be categorized as belonging to 'different' racial groups. Except in the rare case of 'passing', this is highly unlikely in the United States where ancestry trumps colour, and the 'one-drop rule' assigns those with any perceptible trace of African ancestry to the subordinate group.

Recent Brazilian experiments with affirmative action have exposed these complexities and unleashed a fierce debate about the wisdom of such policies. Studies of income inequality in Brazil (Loveman et al. 2012) show that the 'different classification systems yield very different pictures of the nature and extent of racial disparities in income' (ibid.:1479), depending on how one divides the population between those who self-identify as 'white', 'brown' or 'black' ('yellow' and 'indigenous' categories are not included because they are relatively small and reflect the complexities of the actual picture). As the researchers note, 'a forced dichotomous format on official surveys could result in an unintended consequence: the swelling of the white side of the divide' (p. 1476) given the preference for whiteness. Some 44 per cent of brown Brazilians choose the white category if forced to select only between white or black options (Bailey 2009), and this creates the impression that income inequalities are less severe than they actually are. If the ultimate aim is to target those sectors of the population most needing assistance, the issues of whether social policies are based on highly dubious statistical categories, or attempts made by university recruitment panels to determine an individual's 'true' category by looking at colour photographs submitted with an application, become exceedingly difficult and controversial. As Loveman and her colleagues conclude:

> Because race is socially constructed, no set of categories can be argued on the basis of 'science' to be more 'accurate'. Which categories are included or excluded from social surveys or public policies is always already a political matter. And the specific categories that get included can have significant consequences, brightly illuminating some lines of ethnic or racial division and disparity, while rendering others invisible. (2012: 1480)

The fluidity and complexity of the Brazilian pattern of race relations makes it, paradoxically, both more open at the individual level and yet more closed at the collective level: it is possible to achieve social mobility by marrying a lighter skinned partner which thereby strengthens the colour hierarchy in the system as a whole. In W. E. B. Du Bois's terminology, the 'talented tenth' – 'leaders of thought and missionaries of culture among their people' (Dennis 2003: 13) – that vital vanguard of minority progress, evaporates as individuals abandon their roots and accept the validity of the system as a whole. The difficulty of translating American-style affirmative action policies in the Brazilian situation is a clear demonstration of this and reveals the complexity of power relationships in different settings. Paradoxically, the apparent 'openness' of the Brazilian system to individual social mobility undermines the political leadership of oppositional movements in contrast to the 'closed' system of racial stratification in the United States. In the latter case, the only way for political and community leaders to achieve individual success is to change the system itself.

In other contexts: South Africa

The Brazilian case can be seen as a cautionary tale concerning the strengths and weaknesses of a comparative perspective. On the one hand, viewing the patterns in one society in isolation from a wider lens invites a form of short-sightedness that greatly diminishes the value of the exercise. On the other hand, embarking on elaborate comparative analyses without a close understanding of the complexities of each situation generates another type of bias. Nevertheless, trying to place rather different systems within a wider framework has become increasingly necessary as the forces of globalization continue to foster stronger connections between virtually all societies being bound together by the ties of an inter-linked economic and sociopolitical system. The exercise becomes even more challenging when one recognizes that there are 'many globalizations" (Berger and Huntington 2002) and that no society is ever static as far as group relationships, or indeed most other aspects of its structure and culture (Avruch 2012: 93–5) are concerned. In many of the most perceptive attempts to formulate such broadly comparative models of racial conflict – from the early work of Pierre van den Berghe (1978) to Anthony Marx (1998) – the United States, Brazil and South Africa are often the key reference points. But in the South African case, to cite perhaps the most dramatic recent example, a radical redefinition of race relations of a truly fundamental kind has taken place within the last two decades (Stone 2002: 113–29).

From being the bastion of racial oppression under the apartheid regime, South Africa has been regenerated as a society where non-racial democracy is the dominant political consensus. The full implications of this profound and in many respects surprising transformation of a rigid racial hierarchy will be the subject of debate and interpretation for years to come. It has already been the source for many scholars and practitioners exploring the theories and techniques of conflict resolution, and some of the lessons guided the political strategies in Northern Ireland. These in turn have been applied to the continued violence arising out of the Basque region in Spain, so creating an international information exchange and peace network to counter the growth of global terrorist collaboration as exemplified in the case of al-Qaeda.

Understanding the nature of social change, and the extent of its effect on the lives of most citizens in post-apartheid South Africa, provides an important illustration of the dynamic nature of most racial systems over time.[7] It is also an excellent way to develop insights into the generation of racial conflict by analysing those situations where, despite the presence of so many of the characteristics that are often associated with violence, it simply did not take place on the scale and in the manner that most experts, politicians or lay observers predicted. Other parts of Africa have been less fortunate when confronted by racial, ethnic and national conflicts. Some of the worst examples of inter-ethnic strife in the past few decades can be found on the continent, some notable tragic cases being Rwanda and Burundi, the Congo, Uganda and Nigeria, together with mass killings in the Darfur region of Sudan (Horowitz 1985; Lake and Rothchild 1996; Prunier 1995, 2005).[8]

Conclusion: Power, conflict and multi-causality

In this chapter we have explored the changing geo-politics of race relations against the backdrop of two of the most enduring sociological theories used to analyse these issues. Weber's critique of a narrowly defined Marxism and the shortcomings of the equally materialist assumptions of many market-driven theorists have demonstrated the limitations of either approach. Similarly, perspectives that have underplayed the role of ethnicity and nationalism, or the advocates of 'post-racialism', have been found less than convincing. By focusing attention on the recent experience in three major developing societies – China, Brazil and

South Africa – we have shown the capacity of a neo-Weberian, power analysis to better understand the changing patterns of race and ethnic relations in different societies in three separate continents. We will now turn our attention to a central mechanism of group relations, the formation, perpetuation and change in group boundaries, which is a core element in a Weberian approach towards race and ethnic relations.

3

Boundaries

Identity in the New World Disorder

The first chapter of the book set out the fundamental forces underpinning racial and ethnic conflict, and argued that the analysis of power was a critical component in the development and perpetuation of situations leading to such conflicts. By exploring the complexities involved in such an approach, we worked in the tradition of Weberian scholarship that has recognized the multi-causality of all systems of social stratification and the forces likely to challenge the existing order of society as power dynamics start to change.[1] In the second chapter, we further developed the argument by examining the manner in which such shifting geo-political trends are linked to the varieties of racial and ethnic patterns and their constantly changing forms in different regions of the world. We will now scrutinize one fundamental concept that is central to much research in this field, the notion of group boundaries, to see how the strength and permeability of these barriers affect the evolving patterns of ethnic and racial conflict in a number of different settings. This will be seen in the light of the debates that have occurred in the sociological tradition on these matters and will be based on evidence and data drawn from some important contemporary situations.

The focus on boundaries applies as much to states (as well as regional and global organizations) as it does to individuals and ethnic groups. Group social closure, maintaining the strength of the boundary mechanisms, and how these central concerns are affected by global swings in the pendulum between nationalism and cosmopolitanism – inward or outward directions of identification – are all forces actively impinging on contemporary racial conflicts. This can be seen if we analyse nationalist rhetoric and sentiments as they impact many societies around the world, and particularly in the case of the most powerful states. One strand of this nationalist discourse is the notion of 'exceptionalism', found in most societies but prominently displayed in the US and, to an increasing degree, in modern China after the industrial transformations in the post-Mao era (Hou and Stone 2008; Vogel 2011).

The idea of 'exceptionalism'

Ever since the foundation of the United States as an independent state in the later years of the eighteenth century, Americans have come to think of themselves as quite distinct from their European cousins. By the early nineteenth century an increasing number of European visitors were beginning to see American society in much the same light. Gradually, the concept of 'American exceptionalism' started to take hold and received its most persuasive formulation in the writings of Alexis de Tocqueville, whose two volumes on *Democracy in America* (1835–40) became the seminal work advocating this position. Clearly American society was quite different from many European states at this time, but the question still remained as to along which dimensions such 'differences' should be measured. Tocqueville himself emphasized a number of factors:

> The position of the Americans is therefore quite exceptional, and it may be believed that no democratic people will ever be placed in a similar one. Their strictly Puritanical origin, – their exclusively commercial habits, – even the country they inhabit, which seems to divert their minds from the pursuit of science, literature, and the arts, – the proximity to Europe, which allows them to neglect these pursuits without relapsing into barbarism, – a thousand special causes, of which I have only been able to point out the most important, – have singularly concurred to fix the mind of the American upon purely

practical objects . . . Let us cease, then, to view all democratic nations under the example of the American people, and attempt to survey them at length with their own features. ([1835]1956: 160)

While Tocqueville's assessment contained a mixture of fascination and reservations, the 'exceptionalist' tradition has generally been rather more positive and at times degenerated into an uncritical patriotism that sought to elevate John Winthrop's image of a 'shining city upon a hill' to be the model for the rest of humanity. If President Reagan frequently invoked the Puritan settlers' image of America as a promised land, political scientists and historians have been more analytical in their attempts to distil the essence of America's unique qualities, emphasizing constitutional government, individualism, laissez-faire and property rights as encapsulating the core values of the 'First New Nation' (Hartz 1955; Lipset 1963, 1996).

The debate concerning the nature and validity of the exceptionalism label has continued since the Jacksonian era of the 1830s. Another acute observer of American society, Harriet Martineau, writing at the same time as Alexis de Tocqueville, but seeing the institutions and customs of the United States through the eyes of a middle-class English woman, rather than those of a French aristocrat, had a somewhat different interpretation of what made the country so special. For her, it was racial slavery rather than liberal democracy that marked out America as essentially different from most European societies, and while slavery was intimately intertwined with their colonial histories it was virtually unknown in nineteenth-century, continental Europe. As Tocqueville looked with despair at the future of race relations in America, Martineau exposed the hypocrisy of the white Southerners' attempt to justify slavery or, as it was euphemistically referred to, the 'peculiar institution':

I was frequently told of the 'endearing relation' subsisting between master and slaves . . . As long as the slave remains ignorant, docile, and contented, he is taken good care of, humoured, and spoken of with a contemptuous, compassionate kindness. But from the moment he exhibits the attributes of a rational being, – from the moment his intellect seems likely to come into the most distinct competition with that of whites, the most deadly hatred springs up; – not in the black, but in his oppressors. It is an old truth that *we hate those whom we have injured*. Never was it more clear than in this case. ([1837]1981: 33)

Given the fact that Martineau also had a less rosy picture of the status of American women than her French contemporary, overall her assessment of American exceptionalism was far less positive. This complex mix of patriotism, a diversity derived from immigration, slavery and conquest, the impact of a traumatic Civil War, and the uneven expansion of liberal democracy – first to Southern blacks before it was stolen back under Jim Crow, then to women and much later again to African Americans as a result of the Civil Rights struggle – led to the evolution of a society that seemed not only to reflect some parallel developments with changes in Europe but also to reveal other quite divergent features.

Degrees of exceptionalism

If we consider the three dimensions highly relevant to the discussion of changing boundaries and identity – patterns of racial stratification; the role of immigration in influencing the ethnic diversity of society; and levels of nationalism/patriotism – it is evident that the task of comparison is not simple. Once the continental borders of the United States achieved their present-day configuration during the course of the nineteenth century, following the Louisiana Purchase from France (1803), the war with Mexico (1846–48) and the acquisition of Alaska from Russia (1876), further adjustments have been peripheral and connected to American influence in the Caribbean, Central America and the Asia Pacific region. This territorial expansion, closely linked to the frontier mythology which masked the dispossession of Native Americans of their lands and cultural autonomy, resulted in the consolidation of the United States as a continental power. The one event that threatened the integrity of the state was, of course, the Civil War, which despite subsequent revisions was much more to do with preventing the secession of the Confederacy than it was to do with the Emancipation Proclamation. It therefore represented the final struggle for continental consolidation in the middle of the nineteenth century. This interpretation is reinforced not only by some of Lincoln's pronouncements as to the main priorities of the North, but also by the fact that Jim Crow segregation was allowed to re-establish black oppression in the South, reflecting the secondary priority of the goal of racial equality throughout most of white America (Woodward 1951, 1955). Race relations were to remain a continuing blemish on American democracy for another hundred years, until the Civil Rights era of the 1950s and 1960s sought to give meaning to the wider ideals of the American Constitution.

European attitudes towards race relations were mediated through the lens of overseas colonial empires and not by domestic struggles within continental European states. While most Western European states had close involvement in Africa, Asia and Latin America, the actual impact on European societies was largely indirect. Empires affected attitudes of superiority and inferiority, and fed into the pseudo-scientific notions of racial distinctiveness, but barely touched the lives of those who did not spend time in the colonies.[2] Far more important were the inter-state rivalries that were to tear the continent apart during the first half of the twentieth century.

Despite significant flows of inter-European migration in the late nineteenth and early twentieth centuries, these were not generally perceived in the same light as the flood of migrants to North America that took place between 1880 and 1920. To be sure, a few acute observers did notice some parallels and recognized the importance of immigration, which accounted for half of France's population growth during the three decades after 1880. The French economist Paul Leroy Beaulieu commented in 1886, 'France is an *immigrant society* of the same order as the Argentine Republic or Australia. On average forty to fifty thousand foreigners come here every year to settle and take root' (Dignan 1981: 138).

However, this reality was not absorbed into the national perception of what it was to be French. In the American case, the newcomers helped to change the image of the country and introduced a new way of viewing its identity. The notion of 'the melting pot' blending (European) migrants into a new definition of what it meant to be an American started to challenge the earlier assumptions of 'Anglo-conformity' (Gordon 1964). A few decades later, the characterization of the United States as a 'nation of immigrants' could be found in the title of President Kennedy's book (1964), reflecting the arrival of the first Irish Catholic in the White House, and providing official support for the view that America, at the beginning of the 1960s, might fit into a new category of 'exceptionalism', defined as being a member of those few states that considered themselves as 'immigrant societies', celebrating diversity in at least one definition of the term – despite having doubts about Americans of colour – and placing the United States alongside Canada, Australia, New Zealand and Argentina as self-defined (European) immigrant societies.

Other forces were also changing the shape of both the United States and Europe in the aftermath of the Second World War. These were connected to shifts in global power relations that accelerated the movement towards decolonization in the developing world and strengthened the momentum of the Civil Rights struggle in America. Not only did Cold War rivalries open up opportunities for the liberation struggles around the globe, but the issue of imperialism divided the Western allies because of their own self-interests. As Julian Go points out, American power stretching into Central and South America and the Pacific region had many similarities to the previously hegemonic British Empire, even if the ideological rationalization for it was somewhat different (Go 2011: 127). As Go explains, '[just because] America engaged in a new imperialism without colonies doesn't mean to say that it was not colonialism'; in fact, 'the US empire was not a deviation from its British predecessor but a worthy variant that often drew inspiration from it' (ibid.: 66).

European–American contrasts and similarities

While the United States in the twenty-first century developed into an increasingly complex mélange of disparate groups and forces, this was also true for the emerging scene in Europe with its twenty-seven national units. The component states of the enlarged European Union did not share a myth of immigrant origin to act as a benchmark against which to interpret the meaning of recent racial and ethnic shifts. But as the structure of state units began to slowly dissolve and blur, at least on the internal political boundaries of the member states of the EU, this has had significant implications for ethnic and racial relations within the Union, as much as it has for the composition of the constituent parts of the potentially evolving super-state. Flows of migrants that were previously difficult, if not impossible, to sustain have changed the ethnic and racial mix of societies that had traditionally been diversified by migration from the former colonies, rather than by extensive inter-European movement. Two illustrations of these dynamic developments can be seen in the steady, if uneven, progress towards peace in Northern Ireland, and the (temporary, until the Great Recession of 2008) reversal of both Ireland and Italy from being societies of emigration to ones that experienced the economic, social and political impact of immigrants in the tradition of 'immigrant' societies like the United States.[3]

In the first case, the emergence of Brussels as the all-important administrative capital of the EU, forming a neutral pole between London and Dublin, has helped to mitigate the worst fears of both the Protestant and Catholic communities in Northern Ireland that the only resolution of 'the troubles' must be the 'victory' of one side over the other (that is, that the conflict was a zero-sum game). The new political and administrative structure of the European Union suggested that a compromise could work and develop into a genuine 'win–win' outcome. Of course, many other factors have played an important role in this realignment inasmuch as post-9/11 concerns about terrorism have questioned the legitimacy of the traditional support among many Irish-Americans for the IRA

(Stone and Rizova 2007). Furthermore, the economic transformation of the Irish Republic into a 'Celtic Tiger' – prior to 2008 – exhibiting sustained economic growth and high levels of material prosperity, has also been a critical factor in turning a historical society of emigration into a magnet attracting many non-Irish immigrants.

Such side effects, emanating from the similar economic prosperity of the Italians in the later decades of the twentieth century, have also produced an entirely predictable, yet ironic, reversal of attitudes towards 'outsiders', many of whom arrived under the aegis of the greater European project (O'Dowd 2005).

Apart from the economic problems of the Eurozone, perhaps the greatest challenge facing the future of the continent is the relationship between the EU and Turkey. Incorporating a 'secular' Muslim state with a population equal to the size of Germany raises a barrage of new questions about the emerging ethnic and religious shape of the continent. Not only would such a development challenge the Christian monopoly on religious identity, but the internal power dynamics of the substantial Islamic communities – numbering between 15 and 20 million people in aggregate, and located in significant proportions in France (9 per cent); Germany, Austria, Belgium and Switzerland (4 per cent); Britain, Denmark, Greece and Sweden (3 per cent) – would almost certainly be profoundly affected.

While some observers have argued that Muslims and Mexicans fulfil essentially the same functions on the two continents (Zolberg and Woon 1999), we should ask to what extent this is a reasonable assessment. Are the consequences of a minority which is marked out by a distinct world religion, Islam, much the same as those for a minority whose primary boundary is linked to a different world language, Spanish? Bilingualism might appear easier to acquire and a much more flexible option than sustaining a state with more than one monotheistic religion. Does a long and continuous land border pose more of a perceived threat to the United States than the religious affiliations of citizens whose faith is currently being challenged by strong fundamentalist movements? It also raises other provocative questions: will Islamophobia help to reduce the long-standing tensions associated with other types of boundaries by shifting hostile attention away from non-Islamic minorities? Will Latinophobia have a similar impact on the status of African Americans in the United States?[4]

This last question has been further complicated by two apparently contrasting trends in recent years. The election of the first black president in 2008 spawned a larger debate about 'post-racialism' (Fritz and Stone 2009). However, the interesting contrasts between the experiences of different Latino groups, based in part on their national origins and in part on their skin colour, should make any generalizations tentative. For example, the Cubans in Miami (although in this case the obsession with Castro and Communism provided a useful edge over other immigrant/refugee groups like the Haitians (Eckstein 2009; Portes and Stepick 1993)), and the persistence of racial differences between American whites and blacks in health care, education, housing, employment, income, wealth and social mobility (Loury, Modood and Teles 2005; Shapiro 2004) further complicates the total picture. Nevertheless, Obama's re-election in 2012, greatly assisted by overwhelming support from the Latino community, has clearly altered the power dynamics of the situation, and seems likely to change both parties' attitudes towards the question of immigration reform, a central concern for most Latinos.

Islamophobia on either side of the Atlantic

A number of more recent studies have revealed the sheer complexity of the experiences of Muslim minorities both in Europe and America. This is hardly surprising since we are considering a group of co-religionists comprising a global population exceeding the size of China – approximately 1.5 billion in number – and coming from a diverse array of national origins (Pew Research Centre 2009). In her study of the Bangladeshi diaspora, Kibria (2011) explored the similarities and differences between such communities in the United States, Britain, the Gulf States and Malaysia. The contrasts between the first two are instructive since they reflect some of the factors that help us to evaluate the claims of 'exceptionalism' on either side of the Atlantic. First of all, there is the timing of the two migrations that underscore the different historical links between Bangladesh and Britain, unlike the more recent – post-1980s – origins of the American Bangladeshi community. As Bangladesh did not exist as a separate state until 1971, and as most of the migration to the United States took place during and after the 1980s, the dynamics of transnational identity operated in a very different manner in the two receiving societies. Britain's historical links to India and the successive waves of partition, first between India and Pakistan in 1947, followed by the further break-up of Pakistan twenty-four years later, provided a rather different development of the two communities in the two locations.[5] Kibria explains:

> The story of Bangladeshi Muslims in the United States is in many respects very different from that of Bangladeshi Muslims in Britain . . . But there are also many common themes. These reflect the collective memories and understandings that are part of being from Bangladesh as well as the on-going impact of the global national image of Bangladesh on the lives of migrants and diaspora communities around the world. The significance of these commonalities becomes apparent as Bangladeshi Muslims . . . also grapple with the shared dilemmas of what it means to be a Muslim in the world today. (2011: 27)

In other words, a rather different historical context influences the experiences of this particular national group of Muslims when it is in Europe as opposed to North America. European colonialism has much deeper roots than the relatively brief period of neo-colonial encounters between the United States and its overseas empire. Furthermore, the sheer diversity of long-standing connections between the major colonial powers in Europe, setting one state's experience in a very different channel from its European neighbours, contrasts with the similarity of relationships found between the United States and its former dependencies.[6]

This is further complicated by the internal historical legacies which confront the United States and Europe and which influence the debate and actions on immigration policies, concepts of citizenship and the relative responsibilities which arise out of these different historical events. Thus, Foner and Alba (2010) have tried to assess the impact of slavery and the Holocaust on contemporary immigrants and immigration policies in the two regions. As they stress, it is not their argument that 'these historical crimes against minorities have *direct* effects on contemporary immigrants', but rather it is 'the *indirect* effects on immigrant-group inclusion' that they are seeking to explore (2010: 798). Such indirect repercussions are not entirely self-evident and just as the evil history of slavery, followed by a century of vicious Jim Crow segregation, has not eased the path of many immigrants of colour in the United States, so too the horrors of the Holocaust have not made life particularly easy for Muslims in Europe. In fact, in the latter case, and in part the result of the unresolved conflicts in the Middle East, combined with the rising tide of anti-Islamic sentiment in so many European societies, such factors have tended to reinforce both negative stereotypes and discrimination against European Muslims. At the same time, growing intolerance towards Muslim minorities has developed hand-in-hand with a revival of European anti-Semitism, showing how one form of intolerance frequently spreads towards another. Collective memories tend to be short-lived and often one-sided.

From tolerance to intolerance

This transformation has been dramatically demonstrated in the case of Holland in the past decade (Scheffer 2011). From being a bastion of multiculturalism and self-proclaimed tolerance, the society has been divided by conflict and sharp debates about the meaning of difference and the appropriate balance between continuity and change as a result of new migration patterns. The high-profiled assassinations of Theo van Gogh and Pim Fortuyn have also exacerbated the situation. The reluctance of the Dutch, who pride themselves on their tolerance, to face up to these questions is outlined by Scheffer:

For far too long, those who didn't live in the neighbourhoods where migrants settled were the warmest advocates of the multicultural society, while those who did live in them steadily moved out. Their opinions were ignored, or they were belittled for suddenly giving voice to their own latent xenophobia. Now that the middle classes can no longer escape the changes migration brings – in part because they can no longer fail to notice migrants' children in the classroom – the argument has broken out in earnest and there is a need to think seriously about both the life stories of immigrants and the experiences of indigenous residents. It is indeed true to say that the history of immigration is a history of alienation and its consequences. (2010: 3)

Scheffer's analysis harks back to Robert Ezra Park's misnamed 'race relations cycle' that provided a valuable snapshot of the assimilation experiences of the white ethnic immigrants in Chicago in the wake of the 1880–1920 migration waves. Park, of course, has been attacked (Steinberg 2007) for failing to contrast the external immigrant situation with that of the internal migration of African Americans from the Deep South to the Northern and Eastern cities at much the same time. Both flows were interconnected, however, since the old tactic of racial distancing by immigrant newcomers, in order to avoid contact and alliances with dark-skinned Americans, was an attempt to avoid the stigma of association with those at the bottom of the American racial hierarchy. The basic question concerning the Scheffer interpretation of Dutch and, by extension, other European societies is whether a reduction of the flow of current immigrant arrivals will allow for improved longer-term assimilation or whether it will simply exacerbate current tensions, further alienate the next generation of Europeans from immigrant origins, and foster an undocumented underground economy of exploitation, violence and fear that will feed xenophobic stereotypes and do nothing to resolve the underlying problem.

These questions closely parallel the debates in the United States over immigration reform in 2013 where the draft legislation passed by the Senate, to provide a path to citizenship for the 11 million 'undocumented' (illegal) immigrant population, met with stiff opposition from the Republican-controlled House of Representatives. Republican politicians are faced with a difficult dilemma since granting citizenship to this group of largely Latino immigrants will also allow them to vote in future elections and, given the overwhelming preference of most Latinos for the Democratic Party, will make it harder for the Republicans to win at the polls. However, sabotaging the Senate compromise bill may well alienate existing Latino voters from voting Republican in the future and so turn the largest single minority group, who also happen to be living in increasing numbers in crucial swing states, against them.

While the Dutch situation represents a move away from a traditionally open and tolerant society, trends in Germany may be moving in a different direction. In recognizing the future labour demands of the German economy, Chancellor Angela Merkel has spoken of the need to face up to some 'hard truths' concerning immigrants and immigration policy (reported in *Bloomberg News*, 15 June 2013). As a result of projected declines in the working-age population by 2025, Germany will have a shortfall of some 6 million workers and, to remain competitive with the emerging economies of Brazil, Indonesia and China, Merkel concluded that 'we can surely do more to be open to immigration?' Like Japan, Germany's traditional preference for ethnic nationalism rather than civic nationalism (citizenship based on ancestry or 'blood', *jus sanguinis*, rather than birth location, *jus soli*) (Brubaker 1992) sets up a difficult dilemma in a society where trends are leading to an ageing population and low fertility rates, with a resultant diminishing pool of workers to replace those who are entering retirement. The choice is stark: either open up the society to increased immigration, with all its social consequences, as Merkel suggests, or face a future with an ever-declining capacity to compete in a global economy and maintain the generous retirement benefits of a welfare state. Whether Richard Alba's (2009) projections of the possibly benign outcomes resulting from such demographic shifts in the United States – that the increasing power of minorities will force a greater tolerance and acceptance from the dominant society – will apply in Germany or Japan remains an open question. However, one needs to be very cautious when it comes to the future prospects of immigrants in Europe. As Alba et al. have noted:

The problematic status of non-European immigrants is concretized in the inferior and contested position of Islam. Interestingly, even though the French and German states orientate themselves in almost diametrically opposite ways to institutionalized religion, the effects on Islam are very similar . . . Ironically, in both countries, secularism rides high in the sense that levels of religious observance are generally quite low, but this has not helped Islam to overcome antipathy. (2003: 5–6)

Much the same can be said about other parts of the European continent where ambivalence towards the increasing numbers of Muslim migrants has shown itself in Britain, Sweden and Denmark, and has been exacerbated by the terrorist attacks of 9/11 in the United States and 7/7 in London; the continuing conflicts in the Middle East and North Africa; and the economic recession starting in 2008 (Bulmer and Solomos (eds) 2010).

The dynamics of difference

The election of Barack Obama in 2008, and his re-election four years later, are another set of events whose long-term significance has been the subject of much debate. For some, and particularly for many of those who did not vote for him, it represents the advent of a 'post-racial' America in which the ugly history of slavery and segregation is finally a thing of the past. While recognizing its immense symbolic importance, the ascent of a 'black' man to the White House is not regarded by many Americans as the end of racism.[7] In fact, it has been characterized in a variety of manners and for some scholars it is seen as the transition to a new and more subtly elusive situation where the paradox of 'racism without racists' (Bonilla-Silva 2006) simply masks the continuing reality of racial hierarchy in contemporary America. In this way, a new interpretation of race in the United States has meant moving beyond the one-drop rule towards a pattern that is starting to resemble attitudes to race 'in another America' – the countries of Central and South America and specifically in Brazil (Telles 2004). While this more fluid definition blurs the boundaries of racial categorization it may do little to eradicate skin colour preferences in the wider society, or even within the black population itself (Hochschild and Weaver 2007).[8]

Part of the problem is the actual success of the African-American community as far as the growth of a significant middle-class sector is concerned. These achievements, however, represent only a partial fulfilment of the American Dream for a number of reasons. For much of America's black community, poverty, deprivation and a thoroughly unequal lifestyle remains a stubborn reality (Massey 2007) which has only been enhanced by the economic meltdown of 2008. Thousands of young black males are rotting in jails for minor drug offences, in part victims of flagrantly unequal penalties imposed for involvement with crack rather than pow-dered cocaine, and others are struggling with problems that may owe their origins to 'more than just race' (Wilson 2009) but are, nonetheless, anything but colour-blind.

This mixed record of considerable progress in narrowing the gap between blacks and whites in levels of achievement along certain dimensions, alongside an underlying stubborn persistence in racial group disparities, is revealed in a number of recent studies focusing on education, segregation, income, wealth and employ-ment. All of these findings provided a nuanced interpretation of the 'post-racialism' claims made in the wake of the Obama presi-dency. Over a fifty-year period, from 1963 to 2013, significant gains in black educational attainment have taken place, so that while 75 per cent of black adults had not completed a high-school education fifty years ago, that figure had shrunk to 15 per cent in 2013. At the college level, black students aged between eighteen and twenty-four had increased enrolments by three and a half times over the same time period.[9] However, these significant strides in educational progress have failed to narrow the overall racial gap in employment, income and home ownership. On average, African Americans are twice as likely to be unemployed than whites and earn less than three-quarters (60 per cent) of average white earnings.[10]

The evidence concerning levels of segregation in the housing market also presents a mixed picture. Most studies report a decline in segregation to levels unseen since 1910 (Glaeser and Vigdor 2012), with an influx of immigrants and the gentrification of black neighbourhoods contributing to this change, although the suburbanization of African Americans is even more crucial. Nevertheless, this progress in housing integration has been less between blacks and non-Hispanic whites, and more often between blacks and other groups like Hispanics and Asians. Barriers, such as exclusionary zoning in the suburbs and also the decline in the programme of bus transport for schoolchildren, have resulted in some public schools being more segregated than ever, thus contributing to this outcome.[11] So, while only 20 per cent of African Americans currently live in 'ghetto' neighbourhoods compared to 50 per cent a half-century ago, the implication of these trends needs to be interpreted carefully.[12]

The manner in which these changing demographic patterns in the United States are affecting the degree of black social mobility is explored in the report of the Harvard-Berkeley *Equal Opportunity Project* (Chetty et al. 2013). This study examined the chances of social mobility in different American cities and found significant variations. It was revealed, in an interesting confirmation of some of William J. Wilson's earlier arguments about the absence of jobs in the inner cities, that a child born in the bottom fifth of the income distribution in San Francisco had an 11 per cent chance of making it to the top fifth in their lifetime, but in Atlanta the corresponding number was only 4 per cent. The spatial spread of many economically expanding cities in the South and West made it particularly hard for blacks and other minorities to access the opportunities of economic growth because of a lack of good public transportation or other cheap forms of travel.

Furthermore, the recession of 2008, while affecting the total American population by reducing or eliminating their assets in retirement funds and house ownership, has impacted far more severely on minorities. Thus, although the ratio between black and white incomes has remained almost constant as in the past three decades, the wealth gap between whites, and blacks and Hispanics has widened significantly. Before the recession white families were four times as wealthy as non-white families; by 2010 they were six times as wealthy, as measured by assets like cash savings, homes and retirement accounts minus debts like mortgages and credit card payments. In many respects the wealth gap is even more damaging than income disparities since young blacks are far less likely than young whites to receive support from their families to pay for college tuition, start businesses or make down payments on their homes.

Other factors have also enhanced the wealth gap as the housing downturn hit blacks and Hispanics harder than whites. Many minorities bought property at the peak of the housing bubble and after the collapse in the market were left with major debts to repay as prices collapsed. Discriminatory lending practices, involving sub-prime or predatory loans, were twice as common in the black and Hispanic communities than for the white majority, and higher unemployment rates made it harder for them to avoid foreclosure on their mortgages. As the recession has eased, white investors have disproportionately bought up foreclosed homes so that between 2007 and 2010 Hispanic families lost 44 per cent of their wealth, black families 31 per cent and white families 11 per cent.[13]

There are other sectors where apparent progress in improving minority opportunities needs to be interpreted carefully. While the US higher-education system has substantially increased the recruitment of minorities over the past two decades – between 1995 and 2009, college enrolments have doubled for Hispanics and increased by 73 per cent for African Americans but only 15 per cent for whites – these changes mask a growing segregation into a 'dual system of racially separate pathways'.[14] Whereas white students are increasingly concentrated in elite, selective institutions, blacks and Hispanics are mostly attending open-access universities and community colleges. The former receive far more resources to support their studies, are much more likely to graduate and to go on to attend graduate school. The financial consequences of this educational division are substantial as those students with advanced degrees typically earn over 2 million dollars more than non-graduates over a lifetime. A recent report concludes that 'higher education is doing more to replicate inequality rather than eliminate it' in a pattern similar to the impact of 'tracking' students in secondary schools, which tends to offset any advantages of racial integration.[15] By segregating minorities into the low-achieving, 'remedial education' classes, the system adapts itself in a manner that perpetuates the racial inequalities found in separate but unequal, educational institutions.

Some of the clearest illustrations of patterns of race and class reinforcing each other, a theme that is central to Weber's conception of social stratification as a system of multiple and interrelated hierarchies, are shown by the concentration of racial minorities in the US prison system. As Loïc Wacquant has persuasively argued (2009, 2010), this example of what he terms *hyperincarceration* reflects the 'nexus of class inequality, ethnic stigma, and the state in the age of social insecurity' (2010: 74). The reinforcement of class, status and power illustrates the great difficulty facing black youth attempting to escape from the poverty and violence of the urban ghetto. Racial profiling and stereotyping, not only on the part of the police but also by vigilantes empowered by 'stand your ground' legislation – the 'right to shoot to kill' in certain American states like Florida that led to the 2013 death of Trayvon Martin, an unarmed black teenager by a self-appointed community neighbourhood watchman, George Zimmerman – has reinforced boundaries that might otherwise have been declining. After an acquittal verdict in Zimmerman's trial, a *Washington Post*-ABC poll revealed that 90 per cent of African Americans and only 33 per cent of whites disapproved of the verdict.[16]

Furthermore, Wacquant points to the exponential growth in the prison population, from 380,000 in the mid-1970s to around 2.4 million in 2010, and notes that in California alone the number of prison guards exceeds the number of social workers so that 'the state now faces a stark choice between sending its children to college or continuing to throw masses of minor offenders behind bars for brutally long terms' (2010: 90; see also Alexander 2010). Once such a system is put in place, a situation develops where certain major institutions and individuals actually benefit from its perpetuation, such as private prison companies and prison officer associations, which makes it difficult for politicians to rectify such an unjust and wasteful misallocation of resources. The Weberian power perspective can be applied to the manner in which such systems take on a life of their own and, like the ineffectual 'war on drugs', are not discarded even when their utility for society as a whole has been shown to be of little or no net value despite decades of implementation.[17]

Recent shifts in power

Another issue central to the 'post-racialism debate' is the increasing diversity of America's racial and ethnic mix flowing out of the immigration reforms of the 1960s. The growth of the Latino population, overtaking African Americans as the largest single minority in 2003, and expanding more rapidly ever since, poses more questions about the changing power dynamics in the US political system. It has already been noted that some of the greatest beneficiaries of the affirmative action programmes in recent years have been immigrants of colour rather than native-born blacks (Foner and Alba 2010: 804) and, while the demographic forces blurring the colour line of twenty-first-century America may open up opportunities for an integrated society, many would not be as sanguine as Alba (2009) as to the longer-run outcome. The so-called 'birther controversy' – whereby an incumbent American president deemed it necessary to reveal the record of his actual birth certificate in April 2011 – shows the blatant residue of racism even for the most accomplished and successful African Americans.[18]

In Europe, such racist attitudes are tied more closely to the former colonial migrations and to the peripheral migrations from the societies bordering the EU. One major new factor in the perception of Muslim minorities in both Europe and America has been the largely unexpected outbreak of the democracy uprisings in North Africa and the Middle East in 2011, and the repressive reactions to them. Sparked almost accidentally by the public suicide of a desperate young Tunisian – the very personification of the alienation felt by a generation of educated and underemployed or unemployed Arab youth – it spread like a wild fire to Egypt, Libya, Yemen, Bahrain and Syria, toppling entrenched dictatorships and threatening so many others. The fact that these grassroots movements were often led by secular youth, rather than Islamic fundamentalists, nevertheless created circumstances where better organized sectors of society, often Islamist in orientation, were able to (briefly) reap the benefits created by the overthrow of the old regime. This, in turn, reintroduced military intervention, as in the toppling of the first democratically elected government led by Mohammad Morsi in Egypt during July 2013, or a vicious stalemate between the ruthless dictatorship of Bashar al-Assad in Syria and a fragmented opposition supported by a wide range of external actors. In both cases, the complex interplay between power and ethno-religious affiliations can be seen as central elements in the unfolding conflicts.

What the playing out of this wave of democratic revolutions will do to European and American perceptions of their own Muslim minorities remains to be seen, but the unanticipated transformation of the situation in just a few months (not to mention the final killing of Osama bin Laden on 2 May 2011) points to the dynamic and unpredictable nature of much social change. Clearly the secular democratization trends posed an enormous challenge not only to Western geo-political assumptions, but also to the radical Islamist groups (including al-Qaeda) whose theocratic appeal was closely linked to the hypocrisy of the West supporting dictators in the name of democracy. The turmoil in the streets of North Africa and the Middle East may have game-changing implications for the seemingly intractable impasse between Israel and the Palestinians, and the Sunni–Shiite rivalries throughout the region. However, no matter what the longer-term repercussions of the Arab Spring, and they are clearly becoming increasingly complex, they will likely impact Europe and America in much the same way.

4

Organizations

Challenges Facing Global Institutions

So far, we have taken the analytical concepts of group boundaries and social closure and applied them to race, ethnicity and
nationalism. We have discussed *how* the processes of setting and
maintaining boundaries shed light on our understanding of the way
in which power and status dynamics are continuously reproduced
at the level of states, nations and other groups, and how these may
often lead to conflict. In this chapter, we will extend the argument
further and examine some of its immediate manifestations in the
context of organizations, both domestic and global, and consider
their critical implications for the management of a diverse workforce. Managing diversity has become even more important given
the ongoing massive transformation of organizational forms from
the 'old' type of Weberian bureaucracies to a 'new', flexible and
networked form of organizations, arguably better suited to learning, experimentation and innovation. Of particular interest to us
is the application of the sociological perspective on groups, group
boundaries and group closure to the study of race, ethnicity and
nationalism in the realm of organizations. More specifically, we
look at some of the less intuitive, and hence more subtle, social
and organizational mechanisms, which in working together aid
the reproduction of power and status structures along racial,
ethnic and national lines in organizational settings, and hence
carve a space for conflict.

The matter of racial, ethnic and national disparities is of importance not only to social scientists, but also to policymakers and

managers. This is also the case in the context of globalization where organizations, which are truly transnational in form and operation, create salient issues for managers concerning how to respond to what some have termed the 'hyper-mobility'[1] of production, human capital and labour. Under these conditions, managers face employees pursuing 'boundaryless' careers, organizations encountering diversity at all levels and in a multitude of forms, and multinational organizations with an even larger proportion of their workforce made up of expatriate employees.

Is the Weberian model of bureaucracy alive and well?

In the organizational and managerial literature, the management of the workforce, in general, and equity and diversity, in particular, are approached through the framework of the 'employment relationship'. The latter encapsulates a set of practices and rules which govern the relations, exchanges and expectations of both the employer and employees (Ancona et al. 2005: M7–6). There has been little disagreement among scholars and practitioners regarding the social and economic benefits derived from a sense of fairness in the workplace alongside a motivated workforce. The understanding of where these come from, how to make them sustainable, and what their managerial implications are in the context of globalization and diversity have, nonetheless, undergone significant changes.

Ever since the enactment of the 1964 Civil Rights Act and the Equal Employment Opportunity Act of 1972 in the United States, an organization's commitment to federal and local regulations has been regarded as a stable framework for equal treatment and equal opportunities in the workplace. But how could organizational leaders manage effectively the ever-diversifying and geographically spread workforce? In the 1970s and 1980s, the conventional view often saw employees' loyalty, commitment and motivation as traits of their personalities. Correspondingly, the role of the manager was to 'work around' those traits. Since the late 1990s a broader perspective has been taking place, the proponents of which advocate the adoption of a more systemic view. Their approach sees the organization's design, structure and incentives, which guide the daily work patterns, as the critical sources from which employees' motivation and loyalty emanate. As might be expected, the adoption of this view entails significant consequences for managers as they must now regard the various elements of workforce management as 'part of a larger whole', which poses new conundrums concerning the old issues of racial and ethnic diversity, group boundaries and how to manage them in a setting that has become global in all its manifestations.

The larger context within which organizational leaders grapple with concerns resulting from the increased racial and ethnic diversity is best depicted as 'an on-going but incomplete transformation from old to new organizational forms' (Ancona et al. 2005: M7–7). As a result of significant political, economic, social, and technological changes taking place in the past two decades, a 'new' model of organizing the work and the production, as well as the delivery, of both goods and services has been gradually emerging out of the 'old' one. The chief purpose of the latter, which grew out of the era of industrial production, was to accomplish the organization's goals in the most efficient manner possible. This was to be achieved by adhering to the key principles of bureaucracy, as set out in the Weberian ideal type. A clearly defined and strict hierarchy of authority and the standardization of not only processes, structures and skills but also of attitudes, behaviours and expectations were at the core of this model. As the specialization of knowledge areas, skills and tasks grew deeper under the 'old' model, with time managers faced a problem of a new character: namely, how to organize the work in a manner that enabled the 'extraction' of the fine-grained, specialized and, for the most part, tacit knowledge possessed by talented individuals, and to recombine it in new and innovative ways. Since the sharing of knowledge and experience cannot be mandated, the only practically viable, yet not easily achieved, solution to such an enormous challenge was to accomplish this through the systematic and relentless fostering of collaborative mindsets and behaviours at all levels of the organization. To this end, scholars and managers turned their attention, once again, to an organization's form of governance, structure, culture and practices. Hence, the 'new' flexible and 'learning organization' arose as a response to the practical challenges born of deep technical and functional specialization, worldwide demographic changes and migration patterns, technological advances and a clear trend in the developed world towards a shift from a manufacturing to a service-based economy linked to the process of globalization. It compels organizational leaders to succeed through and at innovation by fundamentally altering key features of Weberian bureaucracy, its clearly defined hierarchical structure with decision-making and allocation processes, in search of a framework through which to effectively motivate employees and to mobilize their skills, knowledge and energies. Under this 'new' model, tasks are coordinated not through the adherence to 'fixed' and strictly followed rules and a chain of authority and decision-making, but as a result of collaboration both within and across hierarchical levels, knowledge-disciplines and organizations, and even geography and nations. Although still important, efficiency in this model is secondary to the ability of both individuals and organizations to build and maintain awareness of the types of knowledge and skills possessed by the organization, to continuously search for insights inside and outside of their immediate realms, and to recombine those, turning them into innovative products and services. In short, an organization's survival under this framework is secured through constant learning, knowledge and information sharing across organizational levels, knowledge fields, cultures and locales. Therefore, these types of 'new' organizations are often referred to as 'learning organizations'.

The 'old' Weberian type is best depicted as: (a) *bounded* (i.e., careers, departments and organizations are specialized, as well as being spatially and geographically confined); (b) *hierarchical*; (c) *fixed* in processes and procedures; (d) *homogeneous* in skills, people and places; and (e) *local*. In sharp contrast, the 'new' learning organization functions as: (a) *networked* – both the organization and individuals cultivate and maintain informal and formal connections and thus generate opportunities for collaboration and learning that come from both inside and outside one's area of specialization, department and organization; (b) *flat* with fewer hierarchical levels and more distributed decision-making power, information sharing and actual possibilities for working on high-visibility projects which in the 'old' model were kept only for individuals at specific hierarchical levels; (c) *flexible* in the ways rules and procedures stipulate who should do what and which approaches to use; (d) *diverse* in terms of its work-force skills as well as demographic characteristics (race, ethnicity, nationality, age, gender, etc.); and finally (e) *global*, both in terms of the physical 'location' of where the work is done and, equally important, in its 'mindset' (Ancona et al. 2005).

The transformation from a bureaucracy, as a way of organizing, to a learning organization has been taking place since the 1990s, and some prominent examples of the latter are already in place. Among those are the iconic American-born and based multinational organizations, Amazon.com, an online retailer which started as an electronic bookstore and has retail websites in countries on all five continents, and Apple Inc., the personal and computer electronics firm. Others include Zappos.com, a virtual shoe and apparel store based in Nevada and known for its lateral structure and quick delivery, held together by its quirky culture, and W. L. Gore & Associates, a privately owned company which makes over a thousand products ranging from heart patches and synthetic blood vessels to air filters, and then to Glide and Elixir dental floss, spanning twelve industries. Regardless of their size, knowledge and skill-base, or product and service orientation, what is common in these examples is that each embodies the new form of organizing as a way of achieving the organization's goals.

In W. L. Gore & Associates, for instance, the structure is very flat and the hierarchy is almost non-existent. The organization employs over 8,500 people, has numerous facilities in the Asia Pacific, Europe, the Middle East, and North, South and Central America, and yet its top echelon consists of a CEO and four heads of the four business divisions. There are no 'bosses', no standard job descriptions and no voluminous employee manuals. Employees are referred to as associates and their roles and responsibilities alter over time to match their skills and interests. Leadership at Gore is 'natural' in a sense that one must earn one's followers; a leader is voted in as opposed to being 'assigned to'. The work is accomplished through 'commitments' made to one's team of choice and one's compensation is directly linked to their 'contribution' which, in turn, is decided in large measure by their peers. Communication and networking are tied in a rather direct manner to the success of the organization as a whole, and this cultivates a continual awareness among the organizational members of who knows and does what, and who works on what kind of project. So much so that having a mentor at Gore is 'mandatory', yet no one is assigned one; through deliberate networking, associates are to identify the individual with the most relevant skills set and convince them in the process to become their mentor.[2]

Semco SA, a global Brazilian industrial machinery manufacturing and financial and human resources consulting company, is another quintessential example of a globally spread and networked organization, with a flat hierarchy, flexible rules and regulations, and a diverse workforce. It is best known for its corporate re-engineering which was started in the 1980s by its CEO, Ricardo Semler, who, in his twenties, transformed the company's management style and way of operation from an autocratic, traditional, paternalistic style to a true 'industrial democracy'. Every aspect of this organization's functioning and decision-making is grounded in and guided by the three core principles put in place to enhance the participatory management model. These are the principles of: democracy (employee involvement, yet only based on competency), profit sharing and information sharing. Semco SA – a company with over 3,000 employees who make and sell industrial products and services across the globe – has no receptionists and personal assistants. There are no private offices or reserved parking spots; job titles are flexible and carry little formal status. Employees are not only encouraged to question and to offer constructive criticism of their peers and managers alike but are held accountable to it. They design their products, create their marketing plans and set their production quotas and working hours. Much to the dismay of the outside managers, they set their own salaries too. The organizational structure, known as a 'circular pyramid', is heavily decentralized and flat, with three layers of hierarchy and four titles only. There are six counsellors who integrate the company's moves and seven to ten partners who lead the business divisions. The associates are the people in research, design, sales and manufacturing, and are grouped in units no larger than 150 members. Lastly, there are the coordinators, who essentially are the team leaders.[3]

As these examples demonstrate, under the 'new' model of organizing, information and knowledge travel through internal and external agile networks, and organizations are held together through the 'soft fist' of cultural beliefs and norms rather than hierarchical systems and processes of control. As a result, leaders and managers are presented with challenges of a very different character. For instance, they

> must encourage people to share information and build trust as team members, even as team membership keeps changing in the face of rapidly shifting assignments and downsizing. They have to encourage people with rewards, even as the promise of upward achievement is diminishing, and the new lateral moves and broad job titles are still vague and not as highly valued as promotions. (Ancona et al. 2005: M7–7)

Furthermore, in the context of globalization, managers have to discover new ways of developing, motivating and recognizing a workforce that has become increasingly diverse in terms of knowledge, specialization, age, gender and, what is crucial to our book, race, ethnicity and nationality; each group with their own mindsets and expectations concerning status, authority, respect and mobility, and their own set of beliefs, biases and worldviews.

Since the transformation from the 'old' bureaucratic to the 'new' flexible learning form is not expected to ever include all organizations in all industries and sectors – for-profit, not-for-profit and government – and the traditional Weberian model is here to stay alongside the 'new' one, an added challenge for both contemporary managers and employees comes from the fact that in the twenty-first century people's careers are likely to span several organizations. Chances are that some of those will function more or less as bureaucracies; others as 'learning organizations'. As a result, this places an enormous demand on individuals whose lives and work will be marked by uncertainty and who need to continuously re-evaluate and adjust not just their skills, but also their mindsets in order to succeed in either organizational form and in any part of the globe. In the broader context of globalization and sizeable demographic shifts, it also places the matter of workforce management in general, and the responsibilities of selection, training and retention of individuals in particular, at the centre of managers' responsibilities. Given the uneven economic, knowledge and skills development, though, in the late 1990s the management consultancy McKinsey and Co. described this new reality for managers as 'the war for talent' (Chambers et al. 1998).

The global war for talent

The 'war' represented a new paradigm in the world of organizations – the shift from 'the old reality', whereby people had needed organizations in order to succeed and had sought them out, to 'the new reality', whereby organizations sought out technically, socially and culturally competent employees, as they, with their human and social capital, not technology, financial capital or geography, became the key source for competitive advantage. The origins of the 'war' are found in the worldwide uneven economic, demographic and educational development, which created scarcity. Initially, when the term was first coined, it was used to represent the top 10 per cent of the performers and the ability of an organization to secure such high-performing talent. As the 'war' intensified in the decade that followed, the term became synonymous with organizational practices geared towards the entire workforce and took on a global character (Beechler and Woodward 2009: 274; Stephenson and Pandit 2008). In their 11th *Annual Global CEO Survey*, PriceWaterhouseCoopers (PWC) reported that close to 90 per cent of their CEO respondents identified as their top priority the 'people agenda'; they also stated that it was problematic to find employees and managers with the right combination of skills. In Asia, four fifths of the CEOs reported that a great concern of theirs was the availability of key skills (PriceWaterhouseCoopers 2008: 4).

The current literature on managing talent in organizations has identified four groups of critical factors which at present shape the quantity, quality and the characteristics of the labour force worldwide (Beechler and Woodward 2009). The workings of each of those will, without a doubt, have an effect on the patterns of race and ethnic relations in global organizations worldwide.

The first group concerns demographic trends and the ways in which their effects are experienced given the economic shifts produced by the forces of globalization. The increased longevity worldwide, coupled with a dramatic drop in the birth rates in Europe and, to a lesser degree, in North America, led to a trend for older employees to remain in the workforce longer than in previous times in history. This has created a demand for significant changes in the systems for retirement and health care for the elderly in Europe and the United States. These demographic changes are taking place in the context of increased economic integration between continents, states and labour markets, driven by foreign direct investment. In view of these, in its most recent annual CEO's survey, PriceWaterhouseCoopers highlighted, again, the key themes of concern for leaders around the globe. Not surprisingly, a central one remained the unravelling of the 'talent challenge', particularly when taken in the context of worldwide economic and political volatility, with ethnic and national conflict (PriceWaterhouseCoopers 2014). Its importance is exacerbated by the understanding that, in order to support the growth of organizations, managers need to go global and, in so doing, must find ways to effectively deal with risk while innovating.

The second group of factors that shape the characteristics of the global labour force has to do with the increased mobility of people and capital. The latter is aided by significant lowering of the immigration and emigration barriers in some parts of the world, while erecting higher ones in other regions. According to the United Nations Population Fund (UNFPA), in the first decade of the twenty-first century, slightly over 191 million people, or 3 per cent of the world's population, resided outside the country of their origin. Economic migrants are the world's fastest-growing group of migrants. New patterns of migration have arisen, and many countries that once sent migrants abroad – for example, Argentina and South Korea – are now experiencing migrant inflows as well. Other societies, such as Italy and Ireland, have been oscillating between attracting immigrant labour prior to the 2007–8 crisis, and sending out immigrants after the crisis (O'Dowd 2005). The vast majority of migrants moved from less developed to more developed regions and countries. For instance, the *Statistical Yearbook for Asia and the Pacific* for 2008 reports that between 1990 and 2005, 'Asia and the Pacific, Africa and Latin America and the Caribbean have experienced net out-migration, while Northern America, Europe and countries in the Middle East have experienced net in-migration' (2008: 22).

Given that high-skilled workers have higher emigration rates when compared to those with low skills, specifically, 5.5 per cent versus 0.9 per cent (*Economist* October 2006), these migration flows are also referred to as a 'brain drain' (Tung and Lazarova 2006). Since the early 2000s, another trend concerning labour mobility has been taking place; many developing countries, for instance China and India, are 'luring back' highly trained nationals with Western educational credentials, experience and entrepreneurial skills, who at the same time have retained their knowledge and connections in the local markets.[4] Such migration patterns produce their own effects on economic and social development as well as on the ability of leaders to secure, retain and manage diverse talent.

A third group of factors which exacerbates the global 'war for talent' has to do with the shift from product-based to knowledge-based economies, particularly in the developed world, and the rise of the service sector as the chief employer. According to 2008 data from the International Labour Organization (ILO), about 43 per cent of all the jobs worldwide are in the service sector. In the EU alone this percentage is 71.5 per cent, and, in the US, only 15 per cent of the employees are engaged in 'transformational work', that is, extracting raw materials and converting them into finished goods (Johnson et al. 2005). In other words, in the process of accomplishing their daily tasks, the vast majority of the workforce 'consists of people who largely or solely spend their time interacting – defined as the searching, coordinating and monitoring required for exchanging goods and services' (Beechler and Woodward 2009: 276). As a direct consequence of this shift from a *transaction* to an *interaction* mode of production, organizations must invest in the development of their intangible, human assets as well as in their cultivation and management.

Lastly, by virtue of the fact that organizations operate in an increasingly globalized environment, there is a higher degree of mobility for individuals coupled with a potential shortage of talent, manifested in demographic terms as well as in levels of skill. This requires that leaders of multinational organizations confront the difficult task of managing 'widely dissimilar employee populations, markets, cultures and modes of work' and all the concomitant challenges emanating from those forces (Beechler and Woodward 2009: 276). Furthermore, domestic organizations are also faced with managing a diverse workforce as a result of the globalization of customers, suppliers and investors.

This leaves us with a set of further important questions: how does this global and domestic diverse workforce operate in practice and what are some of the key consequences? Is 'diversity' equally distributed within and between organizations and occupations and, if so, why? Finally, what racial and ethnic patterns of occupational power, prestige and systems of authority seem to persist, and what are the mechanisms through which these are produced and re-produced?

How diverse is the racial and ethnic composition in organizations?

In 2010, according to the Census Bureau, in the US alone, there were 40 million foreign-born individuals, or 13 per cent of the total US population.[5] Of those, about 35 per cent entered the country in 2000 or later. Between 1970 and 2010, the percentage of immigrant workers who were engaged in the US civilian labour force tripled, from 5 per cent to 16 per cent.[6] About half of the foreign-born self-identified as white, 25 per cent as Asian, 8 per cent as black or African American, and 16 per cent as some other category. Of the 47 per cent foreign-born who identified themselves as having Hispanic or Latino origins, only 37 per cent were immigrants; the vast majority of Hispanics in the United States are native-born US citizens.[7] In terms of educational status, 27 per cent of the immigrants who are twenty-five years old and above had either a bachelor's degree or other higher qualifications, while about 32 per cent did not have a high-school diploma. Compared to the 170.7 million native-born adults in the US in the same age group, 28 per cent had a bachelor's degree or higher, and 11 per cent did not have a high-school diploma.[8]

A relevant question to pose here is: how is this racial and ethnic diversity reflected in employment, jobs and occupations? Data from the Bureau of Labor Statistics (BLS) for 2011 show that two thirds of the US labour force consist of non-Hispanic whites, about 15 per cent are Hispanic or Latino, 11 per cent are non-Hispanic blacks and about 5 per cent are non-Hispanic Asians. American Indians and Alaska Natives comprise slightly less than 1 per cent of the labour force, while persons of two or more categories are under 1 per cent.[9] At the same time, about 25 per cent of the organizations in the US employ no minorities at all, while another 25 per cent employ less than 10 per cent (Vallas 2003: 382). In some states, the race and ethnic boundaries in the workplace are even more clearly pronounced. For instance, Tomaskovic-Devey (1993) has shown that in North Carolina more than 50 per cent of all the jobs were held by uniformly white individuals and a quarter of the African-American workers were employed in 'uniformly black jobs'. In their 2006 comprehensive and longitudinal study of the racial and gender segregation in the workplace, as well as employment segregation by division of labour in the decades after the enactment of the 1964 Civil Rights Act, Donald Tomaskovic-Devey and his colleague Kevin Stainback conclude that:

[o]verall, forty years after the law changed to make workplace segregation illegal, it remains high. Most whites work with other whites. Increasingly, white women work with white men. The big success story of the equal rights revolution in the private sector is the integration of white men and women. Cross-race progress among men stalled in the 1980s and among women has worsened since the mid-1970s. (1993: 21)

As to occupations, compared to blacks, in 2010 whites were about 11 times more likely to be executives, administrators and managers (US Census, 2010). About 30 per cent of the professional and related occupations are held by Asian men, 18 per cent by whites, 14 per cent by black men, and 8 per cent are Hispanic or Latino men. BLS data on Labor Force Characteristics in the US depicts the same trend for 2011; a summary version of the annual averages of employment for major occupation categories by race and ethnicity is shown in table 4.1.

In studying the trends in managerial occupations employment between 1964 and 2005, Tomaskovic-Devey and Stainback (2006) found that 'white males' advantaged access to managerial jobs is uniformly high across the entire post-Civil Rights Act period and never declines appreciably ... for craft jobs, white men's privileged access to managerial jobs actually increased in the early period, as all women and minority men gained access to lower-level jobs in the EEOC regulated private sector' (p. 25). At the same time, since 1966 there have been clear gains in professional occupations where, by the year 2000, 'white males' overrepresentation in profession[al] jobs dropped from 45 to 25 per cent. While white males are still the most privileged group in terms of access to professional jobs, that [advantage] has clearly eroded. We see gains for all other groups, except Hispanic males whose trend is nearly flat' (ibid.: 27). Another well-recognized and extensively researched dimension of stratification in organizations is that of distribution of authority along racial and ethnic lines. In their recent review of the literature and study of changes in the authority patterns in the workplace, Mintz and Krymkowski (2010) reached the conclusion that 'no matter how authority is

Table 4.1 Employment by selective occupation, race, and Hispanic or Latino ethnicity, 2011 annual averages (numbers in thousands)

Occupation	Total employed	Per cent of total employment				
		White	Black or African American	Asian	Hispanic or Latino ethnicity	
Total, 16 years and over	139,869	82.0	10.8	4.9	14.5	
Management, professional and related occupations	52,547	83.6	8.4	6.1	7.5	
Business and financial operations occupations	6,339	81.8	9.8	6.6	7.8	
Professional and related occupations (computer systems analysts, statisticians, web developers, etc.)	30,957	82.1	9.1	6.8	7.4	
Architecture and engineering occupations	2,785	84.5	5.2	8.8	6.4	
Life, physical and social science occupations	1,303	81.3	7.3	9.8	5.9	
Community and social service occupations	2,352	76.3	18.1	2.8	10.7	
Legal occupations	1,770	87.0	7.3	3.9	5.4	
Education, training and library occupations	8,619	84.9	9.7	3.5	8.3	
Arts, design, entertainment and media occupations	2,779	87.9	6.0	3.6	9.1	
Health-care practitioners and technical occupations	7,740	80.5	10.0	7.8	6.7	
Service occupations	24,787	76.8	15.4	4.9	21.0	
Sales and office occupations	33,066	81.9	11.3	4.4	13.2	

Source: Bureau of Labor Statistics, United States Department of Labor, 'Labor Force Characteristics by Race and Ethnicity, 2011', at: <http://www.bls.gov/cps/cpsrace2011.pdf>, pp. 20–31.

measured, a variety of studies have shown that, after controlling for an assortment of relevant variables, whites are more likely to exercise authority at work than minorities' (p. 20).

How can these persistent patterns of racial and ethnic segregation and status inequalities in organizations be explained? It will come as no surprise that the preponderance of the explanations link these outcomes to a host of factors. Some are easier to account for, measure and explain; for instance, variations in the attained level of education; the types of occupations and the particular industries in which individuals work; and the geographic areas of the country in which the groups are concentrated. Other factors work in more subtle ways and do not lend themselves to be observed directly, and even less to be measured reliably; for instance, prejudice and discrimination encountered in the workplace.

In his summary of the limitations of the literature on the linkage between racial difference and employment opportunity, Vallas (2003) concludes that the existing studies and explanations have focused mainly on those aspects concerning the allocation of work. In particular, it is the distribution of workers into jobs, in the absence of engaging directly 'the nature of workplace relations, the structure of worker affiliations, and the pattern of interaction that occurs across the colour line. Consequently, the literature provides little empirically-based knowledge regarding the social processes implicated in the reproduction of racial boundaries, patterns of occupational and organizational exclusion, or the formation of informal social networks within and across organizational lines' (Vallas 2003: 393). In the next section, we focus on the role that informal social contacts play in the reproduction of ethnic and racial boundaries in the workplace.

Social networks and the reproduction of racial and ethnic boundaries in the workplace

The questions we will raise here include the following. If old patterns of maintaining and reproducing race and ethnic group boundaries in the workplace persist, how do they survive given the strong push towards diversity by equal employment opportunity and anti-discrimination legislation, the legal protection of minorities, increased migration and demographic shortages? What are the consequences of the racial and ethnic occupational structures for both managers and employees in organizations? What are some of the key implications of diversity for managers?

Social networks and getting a job

Racial and ethnic disparities in organizations have been, by and large, investigated in the context of the social and economic conditions which act as conduits for jobs and promotions among dominant and minority groups (Tomaskovic-Devey 1993). In seeking to explain occupational segregation in the workplace, Tomaskovic-Devey and Stainback (2006) looked at a host of non-institutional factors, such as prejudice, cognitive bias and statistical discrimination as potential sources of racial discrimination in employment decision-making. They found that these 'operate through the flows they produce about applicants and jobs, as well as how that information is evaluated by decision makers' (p. 10) and, in effect, are mechanisms of social closure. The latter involve processes and practices through which in-groups keep out-groups excluded from opportunities. Under such circumstances, the researchers posit, 'desirable jobs [are likely to] integrate more slowly, if at all, as dominant groups attempt to continue to maintain their monopoly over the most desirable jobs, even as they lose ability to control all jobs' (p. 9).

A growing number of researchers have been calling for the examination of the role social networks play in what Vallas (2003) terms the 'reproduction of the colour line within work organizations'. To this end he suggests several fruitful lines of inquiry: 'How do workers "do" race on the job? How might informal patterns of interaction and affiliation reproduce the colour line within work organizations? How have corporate, legal, and judicial interventions affected the character of intergroup relations at work?' (p. 380). In his seminal 1974 [1995] study, Granovetter found that between 40 and 50 per cent of all jobs in the US are secured either directly or indirectly through friends, relatives and acquaintances. In a more recent qualitative study, DiTomaso (2013) found that the percentage of people who rely on their social contacts to find jobs has increased even further. She analysed semi-structured interviews of 246 working- and middle-class men and women from the states of New Jersey, Ohio and Tennessee, and concluded that: 'The average proportion of jobs for which inter-viewees received help is over 68 per cent throughout their careers, with an average for women at about 61 per cent and the average for men at almost 75 per cent' (p. 76). Given these consistent find-ings in different contexts, paying particular attention to the role the informal structures play in breaking down or solidifying racial and ethnic boundaries in the workplace seems indispensable.

Social networks have been found to affect work-related outcomes for individuals both on and off the job (Vallas 2012; Stainback 2008; Petersen et al. 2000), especially in practices concerning mentoring, sponsorship, the transmission of tacit knowledge and employee selection. In the past ten years, Granovetter's (1973) study of 'the strength of weak ties' has been extended to the scholarship on race and labour markets. In this strand of empiri-cal research, scholars have looked at how the social capital of job applicants can be put into use to secure job opportunities for candidates. A common pattern identified in this literature is one in which job seekers resort to their informal contacts (either strong or weak ties, that is, relatives and close friends vs acquaintances) to get information about a job opportunity and to attain a posi-tion (Elliott 2001; Royster 2003; Fernandez and Fernandez-Mateo 2006; Stainback 2008; McDonald et al. 2009). For instance, Fernandez, Castilla and Moore (2000) reported that applicants who were referred for a position by current employees secured jobs at higher rates than other applications. Elliott (2001) showed that Latinos, more than any other group, are likely to secure jobs through a referral by a co-worker. In his study of Asian and Hispanic immigrants, Waldinger (1986) revealed that these two ethnic groups managed to effectively control the access to jobs in a particular market niche – the New York City garment industry

– by using ethnically homogeneous social networks. Fernandez and Fernandez-Mateo (2006) used primary data collected in one racially diverse organization and examined the effects of race and ethnicity in the screening and hiring processes at a factory for entry-level jobs. They found that, generally, whites tended to refer whites for jobs 77 per cent of the time and Asians tended to refer Asians 65 per cent of the time.

In a study of occupational segregation and race, Mouw (2002) analysed data from four cities on firms' 'spatial location' and hiring practices in order to model inter-firm racial segregation. When he controlled for the spatial location of the organization, he found that in firms in which less than 10 per cent of the employees are black, using an inside contact as a referral resulted in reducing the probability of hiring a black employee by 75 per cent. Furthermore, the results from his study show that relying on employees' referrals when staffing blue-collar jobs in each of the four cities increased occupational segregation by about 10 per cent (p. 507). While not in full agreement on the extent of the effect of social networks in job searches on maintaining racial segregation in the workplace, the findings from these studies support Granovetter's thesis of embeddedness (1995) as well as his strength of the weak ties (1973) thesis, while contextualizing them in the literature on race and ethnicity.

Social networks and levels of pay

Another strand of empirical investigations explore whether job seekers who obtain their positions through their social contacts, as opposed to relying on formal channels (e.g. job advertisements, internal organizational postings, etc.), are more likely to secure higher wages, early promotions, higher bonuses and, in general, occupational prestige. A large number of studies have examined these effects in the US labour market as well as globally. The findings regarding the social network effects on pay, though, do not always point in the same direction. While some studies report a positive effect (Granovetter 1995; Lin 1999; Seidel et al. 2000; Aguilera and Massey 2003), the results from others suggest a negative relationship (Green et al. 1999; Falcon and Melendez 2001), and yet a third group has found no effect at all (Elliott 1999; Erickson 2001).

The effect of one's social networks on pay and wages has also been studied for different racial groups. Smith (2000) found that when white males employ weak ties to secure job opportunities, they also secure salary levels which are 7 per cent higher, while the mobilisation of influential ties results in a 17 per cent wage advantage (p. 527). In a more recent investigation, Kmec and Trimble (2009) looked at the relationship between race, workplace racial context and pay outcomes. Their interest was in finding out whether the reliance on social network contacts of different race and ethnicities when looking for a job is likely to result in a different level of pay. To this end, they analysed data from the 1996 Multi-City Study of Urban Inequality project from three metropolitan cities, Boston, Atlanta and Los Angeles (Holzer et al. 2000). Of specific interest to them was an investigation of the following questions. How does the level of influence a contact has in the organization affect the pay of the applicant? To what extent does this effect vary depending on the contact's race and ethnicity? And, finally, to what extent does the racial context of the workplace moderate the relationship between a contact's influence, contact's race and ethnicity, and the level of pay of the job applicant?

Kmec and Trimbe examined five levels of a contact's influence in terms of its strength: (1) a contact with an authority to hire; (2) an inside contact who is a referral; (3) contacts who are not employed by the target firm (outsiders) but provided a referral; (4) inside contacts who were not referrals but did inform the respondent (a job seeker) of an employment opportunity; and finally (5) an outside contact who is not a referral but who informed the respondent about a job opportunity. In terms of their race and ethnicity, 24 per cent of the contacts were white, 21 per cent Latinos and 7 per cent blacks. Of the total respondents in the study, 48 per cent did not rely on personal contacts in their job search. Not surprisingly, Kmec and her colleague found that having a contact with the highest degree of influence in their categorization, namely, one with an authority to make hiring decisions, results not only in securing a position/job but 'yields a roughly 11 per cent higher net pay level than if the applicant did not rely on personal contact use in the job attainment process' (2009: 272). On the other hand, having a contact that is not employed with the 'target' firm yet knows of a job opportunity and tells a job seeker about it, yields a net 7 per cent higher pay level compared to applicants who set about their job search through formal channels alone. These findings are consistent with the results from other empirical studies (Lin 1999; Smith 2000; Mouw 2003).

The question, though, is how the findings relate to the core categories we examine in this book: race, ethnicity, nationality and their effects on group boundaries and conflict. Kmec and Trimble's study offered intriguing insights, which speak to the questions: does the contact's degree of influence depend on (1) their race and ethnicity or (2) their status in terms of whether they come from within or outside of the firm? Through regression analyses, Kmec and her colleague found that race is at play here and that there are pronounced differences for whites, blacks and Latinos. For instance, for white contacts, none of the levels of influence were found to have any significance on the level of pay. When the outside contact who told a respondent about a job is black, though, the results show that this yields about a 12 per cent increase in pay. Similarly, compared to respondents whose contacts were inside referrals for Latinos, an outside contact who told a job seeker about a job resulted in 13 per cent greater pay.

Lastly, the authors examined whether the workplace racial context – that is, if the setting is co-ethnic or non-co-ethnic – made a difference in the ways in which a contact's race, ethnicity and status (insider or outsider) were important. These analyses point to intriguing and, at least on the surface, counterintuitive results, and do suggest that race and ethnic group boundaries are at play. An estimation of hourly wages by a contact's race and ethnicity and workplace racial context shows that in non-co-ethnic work settings, none of the four levels of influence for black contacts are related to pay. For co-ethnic workplace settings, though, the weakest level of a contact's influence – i.e., a black outsider who told the respondent about a job – yields about 33 per cent higher pay for the applicants than the wages of those applicants whose contact is black and an inside referral. As for Latinos, the results suggest that race and ethnicity play a role in the construction and reconstruction of group boundaries at work in a different manner. Specifically, in co-ethnic settings, no gains seem to go to applicants whose contacts are Latinos. However, in a non-co-ethnic setting, having a Latino contact with the weakest level of influence (an outside tie who told an applicant about a job) results in about 27 per cent higher pay for the applicants when compared to those whose Latino contacts in the same setting were inside referrals.

Taken together, the results show that irrespective of workplace context, only the weakest form of contacts' influence seems to affect pay. At first, these findings are a bit puzzling given that an 'internal referral' by definition constitutes a higher degree of influence. As the authors put it, 'they tell us something important about racial dynamics at play in the social network processes' (p. 276). The authors theorize how, given that even when occupying positions of authority, minorities do experience higher degrees of job and social insecurity, it is likely that outside referrals can be seen as 'risk free' for the contact. Furthermore, the results show that 'the only time black and Latino contact-use increased applicant's pay levels was when the applicant did not have a direct contact with the hiring agent' (2009: 276). Hence, Kmec and Trimble suggest that in such situations the positive effect on pay could be explained by the fact that the race and ethnicity of the contact was unknown to the hiring agent and therefore 'not subject to an employer's scrutiny or stereotypes' (ibid.: 276).

In another study of banking and financial exclusion of immigrant communities in the Greater Boston area, Pascale and Stephens (2010) show that the lack of financial integration could be explained not only through the classic lens of looking at the immigrants' individual characteristics, such as levels of education, income, proficiency in English and legal status, but also by paying attention to the geographic dimensions of banking. The researchers build on the literature on financial exclusion and ecology, and examine the spatial relationships between patterns of immigrant settlements in Greater Boston and the accessibility of the ten largest immigrant groups in the area to several types of financial institutions and services. They discovered that poorer and more isolated immigrant groups are disproportionately exposed to check-cashers and pawnbrokers and thus demonstrate the explanatory power of the notions of group boundaries and geographic location. Ultimately, they conclude that the patterns of exclusion are best explained through the interaction of immigration with race and class and that the latter 'creates a complex intra-urban financial ecology of exclusion' (p. 883).

Ethnic social networks have been shown to operate within the Weberian constructs of class, status and power in similar ways in other parts of the world as well. Although the norms through which they emerge, the patterns of their reproduction, the nature of their sources and the elasticity of their boundaries differ, they have been consistently shown to create and sustain patterns of social selectivity when it comes to access to information and opportunities at the individual, organizational and societal levels. Consequently, this poses issues for the managers of private and government organizations and, in a global world, for the development and enactment of employment practice, especially for multinational organizations.

Global perspectives:
social networks, race and ethnic boundaries

Whether they are called *sviazi* in Russia, *guanxi* in China, or *wasta* in the Middle East, we are examining the same phenomenon, namely, the use of informal contacts in virtually all societies as a way of improving one's economic and social circumstances. Social networks are mobilized to match immigrants to jobs in their adopted society, as well as in the native markets. In East Germany, for instance, 40 per cent of the people landed jobs by using personal contacts; in the Netherlands the figure is between 35 and 50 per cent, in Japan about 35 per cent and in China about 45 per cent (Chua 2011). By and large, the networks tend to be based on family and ethnic ties (Portes 1995; Sanders and Nee 1996; Lin 2009; Lin et al. 2009; Smith et al. 2012). In a global world with more or less permeable national boundaries and 3 per cent of the world's labour force on the move, the customary reliance on informal contacts for securing economic gains, social prestige and job finding poses distinct challenges for managing multinational organizations staffed with people from different national, racial and ethnic backgrounds. It also implies that ethnic networks can operate as a mechanism for social closure in global organizations.

In the Middle East, for instance, such practices are heavily influenced by culture, religion, national and global politics. Some recent studies have looked at the critical role *'wasta'*, also known as *'piston'* in the cultures of Northern Africa, have on employment practices in the region and on the functioning of both private and public organizations (Iles et al. 2012). They explore the significance of such factors given that careers in the Middle East, and by extension the management of human resources, 'can be seen as intertwined with international and national politics, legal, cultural, social and economic dynamics, and gender and ethnicity' (ibid.: 467). Studies have shown that in Tunisia and Jordan, recruitment is virtually carried out through word of mouth, or through informal networks, which can enable or constrain opportunities for individuals from certain racial, ethnic and regional groups, and by extension, for organizations.

In the majority of these societies, the social institution of the family is centrally placed even in the economic realm. In fact, it is so vital to society that according to scholars from the region 'it is regarded as improper for the demands of organizational hierarchy to take precedence over the obligations due to family' (Iles et al. 2012: 473). Findings from anthropological and sociological studies reveal that kinship-based *'wasta'* heavily influence each of the managerial processes of recruitment, selection, promotion and decisions on compensation in organizations throughout the Middle East region. In so doing, the existing group boundaries are reinforced as 'kinship, locale, ethnicity, religion, and wealth render some people more privileged than others in obtaining employment, university admission, or equal treatment under the law' (ibid.: 474). Multinational organizations with a presence in the Middle East are attempting to make a concerted effort to institute practices pertaining to the management of the workforce closer to those found in Western industrial economies in order to address growing concerns about a decline in employee morale and productivity. The latter is seen as suffering as a result of a dissimilar treatment of expatriates based on their race, ethnicity and nationality.[10] Among the most needed changes are those concerned with higher pay, training opportunities and measures guarding against discrimination in compensation, promotions and career advancement, while at the same time holding higher performance expectations.

Given the strength of traditional values and customs, one should expect that any of the proposed changes are likely to face challenges in their implementation as each of them goes to the heart of how ethnic, national, religious and racial groups are shaped and maintained. They will affect the manner in which power and influence are distributed and how social status is bestowed upon individuals and groups. In other words, conflict in some shape or form is to be expected to emerge as the proposed practices are likely to shake the established systems of formal and informal power and challenge the stability of the existing order. At the same time, there is strong pressure for higher performance standards, accountability and merit promotions by multinational organizations, which cannot be ignored. To this end, in 2006, under the sponsorship of the Organisation for Economic Cooperation and Development (OECD), the prime ministers of eighteen Arab countries held an initiative on 'Good Governance for Development in Arab Countries' in Egypt. Among the identified critical regional challenges for which policy priorities were set were: implementing anti-corruption and integrity standards, improving scrutiny, increasing performance, and ensuring merit in recruitment and promotion; the results in practice are yet to be seen, though.

As social closure processes are contextual, they can be applied not only at the level of the individual to aid the understanding of how dominant groups keep their power, positions and status, but also to appreciate how these processes manifest themselves in the case of organizational and social change. Taken at a global level, one can look at the ways in which the domination of economic and political elites is perpetuated through subtle, and sometimes not so subtle, forms of social closure. For instance, in the social and economic hierarchy in the six Gulf states that are members of the Gulf Cooperation Council (GCC), and where on average 90 per cent of the population are expatriates, Arabs have the highest standing, followed by the skilled Westerners, then Arabs from other countries, and at the very bottom of the hierarchy are the Asian expatriates, both professionals and labourers. Maleki and Ewers (2007) show that the power and status stratification goes further, and within the group of Asian employees, Indians have a slightly higher standing than Bangladeshis and Sri Lankans.

The social divisions, and even exclusions, are further solidified through lower social and cultural interactions between the local and expatriate populations. Visa requirements, temporary legal status and differences in protection, as well as geographic and housing separation, are some of the commonly used mechanisms to this end. A less subtle form of maintaining group boundaries and differences in access to power and prestige has to do with the 'legal' salary gap between and within expatriate groups. Naithani and Jha (2010) report that 'for similar educational qualifications, work experience and job responsibilities, expatriates from Western advanced nations are paid higher salaries in the GCC in comparison to expatriates from Asian countries' (p. 101). For instance, the 2009 Arabian Business Salary Survey points out that the salaries of the British expatriates in GCC countries are more than two times higher than those of their counterparts from India (Sambidge 2009). According to their data, employees from the UK earned an average $14,500 a month (which also includes bonuses, commissions and allowances) while the average salary of their Indian counterparts was just over $6,000. The highest-paid expatriates, according to the same source, are Americans whose monthly average salary is $19,000, followed by the Australians with nearly $17,000, and the South Africans coming third with a monthly pay packet of $16,152.

Taken together, these data and the findings from the empirical investigations illustrate that irrespective of the type of organizations and organizational forms – 'old' or 'new', domestic or global – the workplace reflects the wider racial and ethnic divisions in societies. In the organizational arena, group boundaries, and the dynamics of power and status disparities along racial and ethnic lines, are reproduced through both formal and informal means, directly and indirectly. Seen in a global context, marked by increased mobility of capital and labour, and a scarcity of talent, such disparities will tend to get magnified and so will the potential for conflict.

5

Violence

Extreme Racial Conflict

In the previous chapter we explored the manner in which the forces of modernity and globalization have had a profound impact on contemporary organizations, both in terms of the way they operate and the challenges created by an increasingly diverse workforce with the need to adapt to new markets throughout the world. On the one hand, previous bureaucratic structures have been challenged by more flexible learning organizations but, on the other hand, traditional techniques of recruitment and advancement have perpetuated systems of racial and ethnic stratification in subtle and often 'hidden' forms that are perceived, at least by those benefiting from them, as 'fair' or merely conforming to traditional values. We now turn our attention to the even more general question of why racial conflicts are so destructive. However, before doing so we need to answer the prior issue of why sociologists, until recently, have failed to give these critical matters the central attention that they deserve.

The study of violence and conflict has often been interpreted in the mainstream sociological literature as being part and parcel of certain sub-fields of political sociology, or those areas like race and ethnic relations or nationalism that have tended to generate a body of research somewhat isolated from the rest of the discipline. There are several reasons why this is the case, which can be tied to the development of sociology at the time of the Industrial and French Revolutions which, although they provided a context containing much inherent violence, tended to look for ways to reintegrate society and overcome the negative consequences of discontinuous and rapid social change encapsulated in Durkheim's concept of *anomie*. This idea of a society uncertain of its central values, creating various types of deviant behaviour like suicide, delinquency and crime, is very different from the massive destruction of inter-state warfare or even the savagery and death tolls of civil wars.

As several writers have noted, this tendency of mainstream sociology to relegate warfare and violence to a side issue is closely tied to the basic assumptions of positivist social science at its outset and the views held in this tradition about modernity (Tiryakian 1999: 473–89).[1] Even though Carl von Clausewitz's posthumously published classic study *On War* (1832) appeared at much the same time that Auguste Comte's *Positive Philosophy* (1830) was setting out the agenda for a world without conflict and violence, the seductive desire to create a science of society that would make warfare obsolete triumphed over the realism that such conflicts would not disappear so easily.[2]

War, genocide and violence in the sociological tradition

Those thinkers who stressed the inherent nature of violence and conflict in society, although often highly popular in their day, have slowly been sifted out of the mainstream in favour of the architects of a new social order or the conservative proponents of the status quo. Even Marx, often regarded as a quintessential conflict sociologist, ultimately turned out to be a nineteenth-century 'progress theorist', whose communist utopia would be reached, albeit after a fair amount of short-term industrial violence and political upheaval. Unapologetic sociologists of conflict and violence – Georges Sorel, Arthur de Gobineau, the Social Darwinists, and George Fitzhugh, to name just a few prominent examples – have been categorized as atypical, generally misguided, and not capable of making much of a useful contribution to the discipline.

One interesting illustration of this process can be seen in the influential writings of Alexis de Tocqueville. No one could suggest that Tocqueville was unaware of political violence in the form of the French Revolution, a social cataclysm that took the life of his great-grandfather and was the subject of his second masterpiece, *The Ancien Régime and the Revolution* (1856). This work did indeed provide some classic illustrations of the power of *relative deprivation* and the mechanism of *the revolution of rising expectations* – insights explaining why revolutions tend to take place when conditions are often improving and not when oppression is at its peak – which form the basis of so many subsequent explanations of violent social change. It is also true that there are some references to race relations in the form of slavery and to the genocidal annihilation of the Native Americans in *Democracy in America*, but this is essentially a side issue from the French aristocrat's major preoccupation with the social conditions underpinning liberal democracy. Interestingly enough, it was his English contemporary, Harriet Martineau, who placed a far heavier emphasis on the racial contradiction to American democratic theory in her *Society in America* (1837), but her contribution had to wait almost another century and a half – for the efforts of Seymour Martin Lipset and the rise of feminist scholarship – before being fully incorporated into mainstream academic analyses.[3]

Some of Tocqueville's most prescient observations on race relations are to be found in his correspondence and particularly his devastating critique of the central thesis put forward by his private secretary – research assistant in contemporary terms – and young friend and colleague, Arthur de Gobineau. On the publication of Gobineau's *Essay on the Inequality of the Human Races* (1853–6), Tocqueville attacked both the basic premises of the main argument of the book and its likely political and social impact, for providing a false justification for the position of Southern white slave owners. Drawing a comparison between Calvinist predestination and Gobineau's racial theories, a full half-century before Max Weber's focus on Calvinism to explain the rise of capitalism, Tocqueville demolished the central tenets of racial theorizing:

> The consequences of both theories are that of a vast limitation, if not a complete abolition, of human liberty. Thus I confess that after having

read your book I remain, as before, opposed in the extreme to your doctrines. I believe that they are probably quite false; I know they are certainly very pernicious. Surely among the different families that compose the human race there exist certain tendencies, certain proper aptitudes resulting from thousands of different causes. But that these tendencies, that these capacities should be insuperable have only never been proven but no one will ever be able to prove it since to do so one would need to know not only the past but also the future. I am sure that Julius Caesar, had he had the time, would have willingly written a book to prove that the savages he had met in Britain did not belong to the same race as the Romans, and that the latter were destined thus by nature to rule the world while the former were destined to vegetate in one of its corners! (Lukacs 1968: 227–8)

This systematic rebuttal of racial thinking – eerily similar to some of the arguments that were to take place around Samuel Huntington's *The Clash of Civilizations* in the 1990s – was confined to the private correspondence between two individuals who respected each other. They simply agreed to differ about the forces and ideas that were to be increasingly powerful towards the end of the nineteenth century and that would be slowly transformed into still more hideous forms with the rise of the Nazis in the 1930s.

Other leading thinkers of the nineteenth and early twentieth centuries actually confronted situations of conflict and violence, but also tended to dismiss these problems as side issues. Marx railed against the evils of imperialism – as did Herbert Spencer, not that it is widely appreciated that the man who coined the phrase 'the survival of the fittest' was, perhaps inconsistently, un-Darwinian when he rejected colonial expansion in passionate and unequivocal language. Who today would recognize the following indictment of European colonialism as coming from the pen of someone that Andrew Carnegie reverentially called 'Dear Master Teacher'?

Now that the white savages of Europe are over-running the dark savages everywhere – now that the European nations are vying with one another in political burglaries – now that we have entered upon an era of social cannibalism in which strong nations are devouring the weaker – now that national interests, national prestige, pluck and so forth are alone thought of, and equity has dropped utterly out of thought, while rectitude is scorned as 'unctuous', it is useless to resist the wave of barbarism. There is a bad time coming, and civilized mankind will morally be uncivilized before civilization can again advance. (Peel 1971: 233)

Quite how this apocalyptic scenario would actually be resolved was left to the imagination, but the underlying message was perfectly clear. The apostle of free-market capitalism was totally opposed to 'the survival of the fittest' when it came to competition between states and nations.

In an equal break with conventional stereotypes, even Pareto, long tarred by the fleeting and highly opportunistic admiration of Mussolini for his elite theories, emphatically denounced the European plunder of the African continent. He too recognized the unethical nature of colonial expansion and the shallow fig leaves – what he called 'derivations' – used to justify the wholesale evidence of violent exploitation. Thus, Pareto's characteristically robust, but clear-sighted analysis of the situation described the outcome and motivations in unambiguous terms:

There is not perhaps on the globe a single foot of ground which has not been conquered by the sword at some time or other, and where the people occupying it have not maintained themselves on it by force. If the Africans were stronger than the Europeans, Europe would be partitioned by the Africans and not Africa by the Europeans. The 'right' claimed by people who bestow on themselves the title of 'civilized', is altogether ridiculous, or rather, this right is nothing other than force. For as long as the Europeans are stronger than the Chinese, they will impose their will on them; but if the Chinese should become stronger than Europeans, then the roles would be reversed, and it is highly probable that humanitarian sentiments could never be opposed with any effectiveness to an army. (*Les Systèmes Socialistes* 1902)

While the final statement sounds remarkably similar to the cynical question attributed to Stalin several decades later, 'How many divisions has the Pope?', as a summary of the reality of colonialism it is not far from the truth. Nevertheless, it is Pareto's work on elites, social mobility and social equilibrium that has received most attention, as his ideas were reinterpreted and synthesized into the structure of social action by Talcott Parsons and other influential functionalist sociologists.

Much the same can be said about Robert Ezra Park, one of the founding figures of the Chicago School of sociology that dominated the discipline from the 1920s to the 1940s, and whose many studies of urban communities and immigrant life helped to shape American sociology during this period. Park formulated a sequence of stages through which immigrants from Europe moved successively towards full membership in the mainstream of American society. Initial *contact* was followed by *competition*, then *accommodation* and eventually *assimilation*. While this pattern provided a fairly accurate account of the experiences of white ethnic groups living in Chicago and the major cities of the North-east of the United States, including Germans, Poles, Irish, Italians and Eastern European Jews, it clearly did not apply to the waves of African Americans who were leaving the segregated South at much the same time and who were not being accepted into mainstream American society.

Park's misleading decision to name the experiences of the white immigrants as a 'race relations cycle' was quite confusing, but should not imply that Park was unaware or indifferent to the plight of African Americans in their struggles for greater equality at this time. Not only had he worked closely with Booker T. Washington (1907–14), the former slave who became an influential, if gradualist, Civil Rights leader in the early part of the twentieth century, but Park had spent much of the early part of his career as a muck-raking journalist before joining the faculty at Chicago at the age of fifty. In his earlier career, Park had written newspaper articles castigating the evils of King Leopold's Congo – a vicious system of forced labour set up by the Belgian monarch at the start of the twentieth century – whose death toll rivalled the genocides of the twentieth century (Hochschild 1998). However, to be fair to Park's critics (see Steinberg 2007), mainstream sociological tools and traditions *did* have a way of washing violence out of the sociological imagination.

There is little in the writings of Talcott Parsons, the mid-twentieth-century sociological theorist whose work, as mentioned above, helped to introduce Pareto's writings to many American scholars, that is centrally focused on race or warfare – the 1965 edited volume with Kenneth Clark being concerned above all with 'Full Citizenship for the Negro American', and interesting for containing a foreword by President Lyndon Baines Johnson. Johnson was, on the one hand, facilitating the historic passage of the Civil Rights Acts of this era amid unprecedented urban riots and violence, while, on the other hand, becoming increasingly embroiled in the devastating war in Vietnam. However, one of Parsons' first students, Robert Merton, did make a significant contribution to the field with his influential argument in an article entitled 'Discrimination and the American Creed' (1949), where he set out the distinction between prejudice and discrimination – attitudes and behaviour – thereby making the case for legislation to achieve greater racial equality rather than relying on appeals to education to conquer bigotry and racial violence. Without denigrating this valuable message from the architect of middle-range theorizing and to a less static version of functionalism, Merton's primary interests remained on other matters. And even his 'radical' colleague at Columbia University, C. Wright Mills, only obliquely addressed these issues through the exploitation of privilege by the military-industrial power elite and some references to Marxism in the third world. To get a clearer picture of violence, genocide and warfare, the typical sociologist needed to step outside of the mainstream sociological tradition and look to the specialist writings of those centrally focused on such events.

Why power matters – indigenous peoples

Racial conflict, then, may be seen as one of a range of group patterns that have arisen from specific historical circumstances. Once set in motion these patterns will tend to develop in a number of possible directions, depending on fairly stable forces. To take one particularly striking example, indigenous peoples have had to face more intense domination, if not outright extermination, when they occupy land (often in combination with other valued resources) prized by more powerful outsiders. Svensson (1978) remarked on this situation when comparing the circumstances of Native Americans and their counterparts in the Soviet Union for much of the twentieth century. It was not that a regime ruled by a ruthless dictator like Stalin had any inhibitions when dealing with potential political enemies or other opponents. The difference was that the indigenous peoples living in Siberia posed little threat to the communist leadership and lived in an inhospitable environment that few Russians wished to inhabit. In the United States, by contrast, from the time of the earliest European settlements, Native Americans posed an immediate barrier and competitive group, blocking access and exclusive use of the resources of the country. Relentlessly, as more European settlers flocked to the New World, the relationship quickly descended into an all-out conflict for control of the land, resulting in a predictable outcome.

Other factors apart from the lack of competition over resources did play some part in the rather different outcomes between the United States and the Soviet Union. One such cultural factor was the incompatibility between collectivism and individualism in the American case, which was much less pronounced under the communist state. Native peoples were inherently communal which set up a fundamental clash between capitalist individualism, a core principle of American settler society, and the dominant cultures of the indigenous peoples. No such problem arose between the collectivist ideology of the Soviet regime so that indigenous communities could be seen as a fine example of 'primitive communism' regarded as the Garden of Eden in the central Marxist texts.[4] However, another important matter was the relative strength of the indigenous peoples vis-à-vis their main enemies. As the remarkable history of the Conquistadors in Central and South America demonstrated, even massive and complex empires could be decimated by diseases to which the population had no prior exposure and hence immunity, rather than simply by small numbers of conquerors with superior weapons. Where indigenous peoples could put up strong resistance, as with the Maoris in New Zealand and the Zulus in South Africa, greater autonomy was preserved and a less unequal outcome often resulted in the longer term.

While imbalances of power have shaped so many aspects of group relations, they do not always fall along the fault lines of race or ethnicity and this is one of the reasons why the sociological tradition has often ignored the racial dimension in the formulation of its major theories. Furthermore, such imbalances are rarely permanent except in the extreme cases of the total annihilation of a people.[5] Genocidal leaders have sometimes seen this as their ultimate goal and the Nazi attempt to exterminate the Jews of Europe during the Holocaust was an extreme version in the twentieth century. While perhaps the most systematic example of the mass murder of a particular group, even this horrific case is but one of a series of massacres perpetrated during the century. Hitler himself made the cynical comment, 'Who remembers the Armenians?', in reference to the apparent indifference of so many societies to earlier examples of widespread group killings, this time referring to the 1.5 million victims of the chaos and collapse following the end of the Ottoman Empire between 1915 and 1923. The critical issue for social scientists is less the fact that certain leaders are capable of advocating such draconian measures than that so many 'ordinary people' are prepared to participate in or remain indifferent to such horrors. One plausible explanation for this is to link these actions to the forces of modernity that seem to promote the 'banality of evil' (Arendt 1964; Katz 1993), where killing on a factory basis is seen as involving groups of dedicated bureaucrats, albeit often instructed by a few psychopaths, simply 'doing their jobs'. However, the participation of thousands of machete-wielding killers in the Rwandan massacres of 1994, or among the fanatical Khmer Rouge followers of Pol Pot in the Cambodian killing fields between 1975 and 1979, suggests that modernity is neither a necessary nor a sufficient explanation for these actions.

The reason why so few of the classic texts of sociology are directly concerned with such a critical feature of modern society, the lives and deaths of millions, is not difficult to understand. Social science in its modern form developed out of the political upheaval of the French Revolution and the radical economic changes of the Industrial Revolution. Neither great transformation was directly couched in terms of racial or ethnic conflict. Thus, the pioneers of sociology were obsessed by issues of social order and its disruption, of the impact of industrial society on social stratification, and the desire to incorporate the notion of progress into a new world order based on rationality and science. There is very little in the work of Saint-Simon and Comte, Spencer and Marx, or Weber and Durkheim that focuses *centrally* on the issues of race and ethnicity, even if some of their concepts could be and were adapted to understanding these questions.

This does not mean that during the nineteenth and early twentieth centuries, race relations and racial conflict were unimportant; they were not. It is merely that the key thinkers in this field were primarily interested in other issues. Much the same can be said of feminist perspectives and causes that were similarly relegated to secondary status, despite the important work being done in these realms. The explanation for this lies in several causes central to the sociology of knowledge, which once again links the power structure not so much to the generation of ideas but to their propagation and dissemination.[6] Only in the second half of the twentieth century did major shifts in the global power structure lead to the re-evaluation of the importance of thinkers such as W. E. B. Du Bois and Harriet Martineau for an understanding of society and social change following in the wake of decolonization, the Civil Rights struggle, and the suffragette and feminist movements.

Bringing violence back in

There were, of course, strands of work within the social sciences that did take violence, war and genocide as something more than the aberrations of a social system that was temporarily out of equilibrium. Most of this work was concerned with specific acts of violence, systems that seemed to depend on violence for their survival, and scholarship concerning the undeniable outcome of naked violence. Many of the consensus/functionalist sociologists did start off their analysis from the 'Hobbesian problem of order' where life was 'nasty, brutish and short', but the continual emphasis on ways to solve this conundrum seemed to underplay the continuing significance of violence in so many social relationships. The lynch mobs of the Jim Crow era terrorized black Americans and helped to prevent any large-scale challenges to the reimposition of Southern white supremacy; the pass laws and the apartheid legislation in South Africa between 1948 and 1990 set up a racial police state to violently oppress any opposition; the police, military and the Protestant militias served the same functions in keeping the Catholics of Northern Ireland in a subordinate political position until the outbreak of 'the troubles' at the end of the 1960s; while the nationalist parties and leadership throughout the former Yugoslavia sought to create ethnic hegemonies during the political power vacuum of the post-Soviet Balkans. None of these situations fitted easily within the standard models of the sociological tradition, so scholars wishing to place such violence and conflict at the centre of their analyses needed to shift their attention to the fields of nationalism and race relations.

Scholarship on ethno-nationalism and research on race relations intersect in important and interesting ways (Conversi 2004). Although nationalism is often associated with regions of the world possessing long-established state systems, like Europe, Japan and China, the scholarship on ethnic and racial conflict tends to focus more prominently on the societies of immigration, like the United States, Canada, Argentina and Australia. The developing regions of Africa and many parts of Asia and Latin America fall somewhere between the two. However, like so many crude generalizations, this one tends to fall apart on closer examination for the simple reason that there are so many exceptions that undermine the utility of the divisions. Such a conclusion is reinforced as we consider some of the special characteristics of the evolving world in the twenty-first century: the hegemony of global capitalism; the changing nature of migration that takes on a variety of forms in addition to the major South–North movements – transnationalism, diasporas, illegal migration and professional multiple migrants, to cite just a few examples – and the new trends in industrial production, commercial relationships and financial networks that are reshaping the power realities of modern global society. Nevertheless, other forces are being generated that represent counter-reactions to these wider developments: anti-globalization alliances, social movements that seek to restore traditional values increasingly being threatened, if not undermined, by the impact of post-modernity, and fundamentalist religious and political mobilization that attempts, in a similar manner, to challenge the direction of global inequality in an era when the nation-state is either considered to be an anomaly or a total anachronism.

Within this wider framework, new emerging patterns of race and ethnic relations are developing in a complicated manner that defies simple explanations. If the way we treat each other depends on the basic distribution of power resources among individuals, at the micro-social level, and among groups, at the macro-societal level, then a key to understanding these new patterns lies in charting the redistribution of global power in all its many manifestations.

Race relations and nationalism

Just as the field of race relations has undergone significant changes in the post-Cold War era, so much of the scholarship on nationalism has also altered significantly as a result of the same structural, political and cultural transformations associated with the geopolitical shifts of the decades surrounding the new century. A stable bipolar military stalemate until 1989 made way for the dominance of a single superpower, the United States, with all the consequences that could be predicted from such an unbalanced concentration of power. The break-up of the former Soviet sphere of influence and the revitalization of nationalism and religion in many of the former satellite states of the USSR, to fill the vacuum left by a discredited ideology and a crumbling economic system, has seemed to vindicate Walker Connor's prediction that 'when the chips are down' nationalism would trump socialism in much of the communist bloc (Connor 1984, 1994). At the same time, the spread of unfettered capitalism in systems ill-prepared for such a dramatic change of economic gears has resulted in huge disparities of wealth and income, and the corresponding political counter-movements resulting from the *anomie* and alienation of massive social dislocation. Furthermore, in the case of China, a global industrial revolution of truly historic proportions has been affected by the uneasy coalition of rampant capitalist production and sustained centralized political control, challenging the conventional wisdom of so much Western political, economic and social theory that free markets and liberal democracy inevitably go together.

The field of nationalism in the twenty-first century is still the object of a major debate about the ethnic origin of nations and the so-called 'primordial versus constructivist' controversy continues to persist. Anthony Smith's influential studies (2003, 2004) document the 'antiquity of nations' and argue that the common theme of 'chosen peoples' is often linked to the sacred sources of national identity. He suggests that 'pure "invention of tradition"' is likely to be ineffective in the longer run (2004: 230) and notes:

> [W]e speak readily of an age of nations and nation states succeeding one of feudal or tribal kingdoms and superseded by one of continental unions or of globalization. But these are blanket evolutionary terms, extrapolated from one region of the globe to others, which fail to differentiate between different examples and varied cultural areas of 'strong' and 'weak' national identities, just as they tend to overgeneralise the extent and depth of continental or global interdependence . . . Above all, we need to reconsider the place of the sacred in a secularizing world. (2003: 261)

Other scholars of nationalism have shifted the debate from the 'when is a nation' theme to include more elaborate discussions of the consequences, as much as the origins, of ethnonationalism and ethnosymbolism (Leoussi and Grosby 2007). Thus John Hutchinson (2005) has focused on the differences between 'hot' and 'banal' nationalisms and how they contribute to our understanding of nations as 'zones of conflict'. However, he also argues that 'what we call globalization in the contemporary period is likely to lead to the intensification of nationalism and national identities rather than to their erosion' (2005: 7).

Another study with a related message is Michael Mann's *The Dark Side of Democracy* (2005). Mann revives many of the issues explored by Leo Kuper in the early 1980s (1983, 1985) by examining the nature of ethnic cleansing and analysing the dynamics of genocide. This scholarship fits within the tradition of research pioneered by Hannah Arendt's famous insight, derived from her observations of the Eichmann trial in Jerusalem, into the 'banality of evil' and this has been elaborated on by such scholars as Fred Katz (1993, 2004) and Jessica Casiro (2006, 2010). The structural 'normalcy' of so much evil, as well as a surprising amount of 'altruism', according to Casiro's case study of rescuers during the Argentine junta's repression between 1976 and 1983, provides grounds for both continuing concern but also for some hope for the future. If routine patterns of social organization and individual behaviour can lead to such horrific outcomes, then it is equally plausible that fairly mundane strategies may prove to be an effective antidote to them as well.

A number of studies of nationalism outside the European background provide us with further insight into its interface with ethnic and racial diversity. Jonathan Eastwood's research on the early rise and crystallization of nationalism in Venezuela traces a development towards a pattern of civic nationalism, rather than ethnic nationalism, which is clearly based on the French model. As he also points out, the Venezuelan variety of nationalist sentiment was collectivist and not individualistic in character, generating a political culture that 'remains potentially predisposed to authoritarianism' (2006: 154).[7] However, an interesting consequence of this conceptualization is that despite documented 'discrimination against those of indigenous or African ancestry over various periods in Venezuelan history ... one is no less Venezuelan for being indigenous or black or, for that matter, of Spanish or even German ancestry' (ibid.).

So much of the writing and research in both fields, race relations and nationalism, emphasize how the developments in global society have impacted the traditional divisions between groups, and created new bases for social cohesion and conflict. The switch between the Cold War assumptions of a bipolar world to the subsequent reality of a single superpower, quickly over-reaching itself and generating unintended consequences from its unilateral intervention in the Middle East, establishes a different environment in which both nationalism and race relations are being played out. By pursuing strategies that reflect its unrivalled military supremacy, the government of the United States under the Bush Administration slowly learned the limits of 'hard' power.[8] Attempting to solve political and 'ethno-sectarian' conflicts by involving soldiers against insurgent terrorist violence, taking place in an urban civilian environment, is a policy that rarely succeeds and often creates more, rather than less, conflict.[9]

This is not to suggest that geo-political change is a sufficient explanation to account for much ethnic conflict and many other factors at a lower level often must interact in a certain pattern before the absence of structural restraints leads to violence and degenerates into genocidal massacres (Mann 2005: 418–27; Sekulić et al. 1994, 2006).[10] Much the same dynamic interaction of power has resulted from the removal of Saddam Hussein's Ba'athist – Sunni, minority-dominated – regime in Iraq. The fall of the dictator has created a power vacuum in which the interests of Shiites, Sunnis and Kurds are seen by many as a competitive, zero-sum game, and one in which the strategic interests of external political and military forces, including those emanating from Iran, Saudi Arabia, Syria and Turkey, complicate the picture far beyond the initial assumptions and plans of the United States and its allies. This situation demonstrates both a remarkable failure not only to understand the subtle cultural and structural preconditions of 'democracy' even under the best of circumstances – did Tocqueville write in vain? – but also a cavalier disregard for the further complications generated by ethno-sectarian divisions that would challenge and strain even well-established democratic political cultures. The shift of goals from a messianic movement for Muslim democratization, to creating a minimum semblance of stability to allow the various parties to negotiate any type of non-violent settlement, reflects the playing out of these forces.

Other solutions turn to the many forms of federalism that have been adopted by multi-ethnic and religiously diverse societies to moderate and contain group competition and conflict. But again, the limitations of these approaches, and the often unique circumstances that allow them to function, are too often unappreciated. One only has to remember the characterization of Lebanon in the 1960s as the 'Switzerland of the Middle East'. This was a society that had achieved an internal balance between its diverse religious and ethnic groups by sharing power on an equitable basis. However, the situation was utterly transformed by the subsequent conflicts between Israel, Syria, the PLO and Hezbollah, which polarized the Lebanese communities and led to civil war and continuing hostilities. To understand the fragility of such arrangements is to appreciate their dependence on the tacit agreement of powerful neighbouring states to allow the federal bargain to persist.[11]

That said, it must also be recognized that there seems to be a constant dialectic of fusion and fission operating in the global environment, with the collapse of the Soviet system in Eastern Europe being followed by the continuously expanding European Union in the subsequent two decades. No one could claim that the component parts of the EU have not shared a particularly violent history of inter-state and inter-ethnic conflicts stretching back centuries, yet the pull of the European ideal has not only drawn in the twenty-seven members, as of 2012, but is also an attractive option for Croatia and Serbia and, above all, Turkey.[12]

Ethnic violence: causes and consequences

Another important issue is the extent to which racial and ethnic polarization precedes or is largely caused by violence and war. In some cases, both causal factors may be in play, but in others the actual brutality of the conflict seems to be a primary explanation of the redefinition of neighbours as enemies. The degree to which this is brought about by the manipulation of cynical elites, or generated at the mass level, is another issue that demands careful empirical investigation. Playing the 'race card' or bowing to popular xenophobic prejudice, suggests two rather different political strategies that may create very different long-run dynamics. This parallels the distinction found in Simmel's classic analysis of conflict between *divide et impera* and *tertius gaudens*, between those who exploit existing divisions for their own advantage and those who actively promote them for the same ends (Wolff 1950: 154–69). Similarly, nationalism by manipulation and nationalism through conviction may not follow entirely the same paths, and in most actual cases manipulation and conviction are present in varying degrees at both the elite and the mass levels.

A third factor of note concerns the continuing shifts in power relations and group definitions that constantly occur as the result of social and political change. Most studies include geo-political transitions as essential elements influencing the nature and variety of inter-group relations. Thus, the end of the Cold War, the impact of globalization on migrant movements influencing the ethnic diversity of societies, the consolidation and the formation of new power blocs, and the influence (or lack of it) of international organizations,[13] all have an impact on racial and ethnic conflict. Furthermore, important changes are taking place within societies, producing a number of policy shifts. The development of plans in South Africa and Brazil to institute affirmative action policies, and the decisions of Malaysia and the US to abandon or severely curtail their own, reflect constantly changing power realities in different parts of the world. As we will explore in the final chapter, such policies may alter the power balances in a society over time, but their implementation will also be subject to the strength of the parties involved and how they perceive the costs and benefits of these strategies for themselves, as well as for society as a whole.

Conclusion: mainstreaming the problems of violence and peace

From this brief survey of some of the emerging trends in both the sociology of race relations and nationalism, a few general conclusions emerge. First is that single explanations relying on a dominant cause only occasionally account for the complexity of actual events. This fits in with the neo-Weberian tradition that is the central thread of our analysis, though major differences in class, status and power – Weber's classic dimensions of social stratification – tend to act as a general basis of conflict and violence when superimposed on ethnic or racial groups. However, these are necessary, but rarely sufficient, causes of racial or nationalist mobilization. In most cases it is the occurrence of changes, or the *perceived* fears of possible changes in racial or ethnic privilege, or the *perceived* hopes that liberation or greater equality may at last be possible, which act as the spark and lubricant of hostility and conflict. Thus, models used by social scientists to analyse, and ultimately to predict, riots, expulsions, genocidal massacres and other forms of ethnic, racial and nationalist conflict all contain elements of truth but rarely the whole truth. So in the case of the break-up of Yugoslavia, or in the relatively peaceful democratic transition in South Africa, both of which we will consider in more detail in chapter 6, or the final stages of a resolution of sectarian violence in Northern Ireland, multiple factors operating at several levels need to be added to the explanation. Consequently, a variety of perspectives often incorporate arguments which are persuasive in particular situations, but the more interesting questions frequently involve the manner in which these different forces interact with each other to produce a given outcome.[14]

A final point that needs to be stressed is that while conflicts among racial and ethnic groups are a constant feature of human societies, they are by no means inevitable. As Donald Horowitz noted some three decades ago, 'ties of blood do not lead ineluctably to rivers of blood' (1985: 684). For long periods of time, diverse racial and ethnic groups can live together in relative harmony, or conflicts may be structured along different channels, with individuals aligning themselves as members of collectivities that are not defined by racial or ethnic boundaries, such as class, age or gender. The important issue for social scientists is to recognize the dangerous potential of ethnic and racial divisions – barriers that are shared by all mankind – and to explore the ways in which they can be institutionalized in non-lethal directions. We will turn to these questions in more detail in the final chapter.

6

Justice

The Search for Solutions

Given the levels of global racial and ethnic conflict, our final chapter seeks to explore several of the more common remedies that have been suggested to address some of these issues. As our earlier discussion has suggested, the elimination of all forms of group conflict, whether based on racial, ethnic or national boundaries, is neither feasible nor even desirable. Too many of the utopian solutions in the past have proven to be more destructive and created greater suffering than the conflicts they claim to have resolved. However, this should not lead to a sense of fatalism – that nothing can be done to rectify the crimes committed by those seeking to promote the superiority of one group over another in the myriad forms of domination and destruction that cover the pages of the history books.

A number of different levels of approach can be evaluated and if the perfect solution does not exist in the real world, as is so often the case, then a variety of strategies – realistically appreciating the relevance of power and the differential access to resources that the neo-Weberian approach emphasizes – can be assessed. This brings us to consider the latest phase of global political struggle that may be seen from a range of different perspectives. Just as the economic readjustments at the end of the twentieth century seemed to mirror the expected outcome of the collapse of communism, the political trends appeared to follow a rather more complex and, in several cases, a quite different logic. Variations on the theme of global capitalism have become almost universal, but the political consequences are by no means universal. While low-level terrorism has been a continuous feature of much of the history of the twentieth century, the spectacular attack in September 2001 on the World Trade Center in New York and the Pentagon near Washington suggested an altogether new phase in global political conflict. Paralleling the rise of the non-state power of the modern multinational corporation, fundamentalist suicide bombers appeared to be operating in a very different arena than the largely localized struggles for national autonomy and independence of the IRA, Basque separatists or the Tamil Tigers. Global terrorism was just that – *global* – with loose-knit cells capable of inflicting enormous death and destruction outside the conventional barriers of inter- or sub-state rivalries. Perhaps even more disruptive than the actual loss of life were the reactive methods employed to 'respond' to the threats, which impacted on the everyday lives of the citizens of the targeted states.

Was this the vindication of what Samuel Huntington had been suggesting as a logical outcome of the end of the ideological struggle of the Cold War, and, if so, what were the likely consequences as far as traditional forms of racial, ethnic and national conflict were concerned? Would the war on terrorism create totally new alliances capable of trumping the traditional divisions and tensions between racial, ethnic and national groups? Certainly, both the United States and much of Western Europe had Muslim minorities that could be demonized, seen as being part of an irrational fundamentalist plot to reject 'Western' materialism, secularism and democratic values. The rise of Islamophobia – which made the implausible claim that the billion Muslims of the world, rather than small groups of militant minorities, formed a threat to the rest of humanity – might substitute Muslims as a new 'axis of evil', replacing the earlier capitalist–communist rivalry with a convenient enemy for those missing a scapegoat for the complex frustrations of modern life. However, this worldview quickly falls apart when the alliances between the Saudi ruling family and the United States, or between Turkey and NATO, and so many other cross-religious forms of cooperation fail to fit such a simplistic model.[1]

So, if terrorism has significantly influenced the lives of many people throughout the world, does it in any way alter the structural divisions that were so prominent prior to 9/11? There is little evidence that this is the case, with the war on terrorism supplementing or reversing the types of trends associated with globalization. The impact of Hurricane Katrina, providing images of the stark racial poverty in a flooded New Orleans, not to mention the lack of urgency in reacting to the crisis, merely brought to the attention of a wider American public the message that so many academic studies have continued to underline. Poverty in America is still inextricably linked to race and this is true whether one looks at housing segregation patterns (Massey and Denton 1993), educational underachievement and re-segregation (Kozol 2005), or income and wealth distribution (Shapiro 2004). Despite the election victory of Barack Obama in 2008, and his re-election in 2012, which was of course of great symbolic importance, the underlying structural inequalities of the American economy still remain and the Great Recession of 2008 has certainly not helped in producing greater racial and ethnic equality. Furthermore, the slow but determined attrition of affirmative action policies has tended to diminish any narrowing of the racial gap. The sub-prime housing loan catastrophe has disproportionately affected black and other minority homebuyers. In Europe, similar trends have retarded the assimilation of new and established migrant groups and slowed the egalitarian directions of the European Union (Loury, Modood and Telles 2005).

Another area where the war on terrorism may have affected the ability of global institutions to belatedly react against pressing inter-racial and inter-ethnic crises is in the ultimate violence of genocide. For most of the twentieth century, the record of attempts to prevent the millions of deaths resulting from a succession of genocides has been dismal. The butchery in the Belgium Congo at the start of the century, the Armenian genocide in 1915, the slaughter of 6 million Jews in the Holocaust, the mass killings in Cambodia and Rwanda in the later decades of the century, reveal the continual failure of any effective global response designed to monitor and intervene in such flagrant examples of mass murder

(Hochschild 1998; Balakian 2003; Weitz 2003). More recent developments in the war on terrorism have further undermined any systematic and effective response. By side-stepping the Geneva Convention on torture, the legitimacy of international institutions to send a basic message about the minimal protections of human rights has been gravely compromised. In addition, the unilateral action of the United States and Britain to wage war in Iraq has also further weakened the growth of multilateral cooperative strategies designed to address many of the world's most urgent problems associated with ethnic, racial and religious conflict and violence.

While subsequent action in Libya during the Arab Spring of 2011, and the conviction of the former Liberian leader, Charles Taylor, for crimes against humanity in the International Criminal Court in 2012, represent some progress, the refusal of major powers like Russia and China to 'interfere in the internal affairs of a sovereign state', during the Syrian uprising, illustrates many of the limits of global action. If globalization has generated conditions and reactions that present a new phase of conflict between these groups, it would seem that this has created both opportunities and problems in equal measure. Trying to understand the dynamics and long-term significance of these processes is the challenge facing scholars of race and ethnic relations for the next few decades.

Justice and affirmative action

If one of the central problems posed by diversity is linked to inequality in all spheres of life, what then are some of the possible strategies that may help ameliorate this situation? Let us start with a highly controversial set of policies that have been tried in a number of different societies in a variety of forms for more than a century. Although affirmative action is associated by many with the policies that emerged in the United States during the 1970s after the initial phase of the Civil Rights movement had revealed the enormous disparities in education, income and lifestyles that would not be addressed by the important, but limited, step of legalizing equal rights, preference policies for underprivileged groups have a much longer history. Preference for dominant groups is inherent in all forms of racial and ethnic discrimination and we will consider the re-evaluation of these entrenched privileges in our discussion of the fierce debates between proponents who stress equal opportunities, as opposed to those who advocate the merit of equal outcomes.

Of all the states in the modern world, India has the longest experience of preference policies, dating back to the end of the nineteenth century. In 1895, certain government jobs in Mysore in southern India were reserved for the so-called 'backward' castes, initiating the first quota system on the subcontinent. In 1915, in Travancore, in what is now southern Kerala state, specific jobs were reserved for various 'untouchable' groups and, in 1942, the British colonial administration imposed an 8.5 per cent quota for what it termed 'depressed classes', which was expanded to 12.5 per cent, a figure corresponding to their proportion in the population, four years later. After independence in 1947, 12 per cent of government jobs were reserved for former 'untouchables' and 5 per cent for indigenous tribal peoples. These quotas were then incorporated into the 1950 Constitution. Subsequently, two important rulings have taken place to clarify and refine the operation of the system. In 1984, a lower court rejected quotas for poor members of upper castes on the grounds that despite their poverty they could not be 'socially and educationally backward'. In 1992, the Supreme Court ordered a 27 per cent quota for the 'socially and educationally backward', but excluded the more prosperous members of such groups. It also capped overall quotas for disadvantaged groups, if they exceeded 70 per cent of a given population, at no more than 50 per cent.

The debates in India are in many respects similar to the controversies in the United States about these issues.[2] Questions are being asked as to how long a time it might be legitimate to retain quota systems; whether the skewed class benefits of a group preference approach can be justified; and if alternative strategies for alleviating poverty should not be given higher priority in public policy. Evidence towards the end of the twentieth century suggested that affirmative action had at least diversified the growing middle class, with estimates that 20–25 per cent of this economic group came from lower castes (Sheth 1997). Subsequent research has revealed the enormous problems facing policies that attempt to promote greater equity when group boundaries are often unclear and continually changing over time (Deshpande 2006; Yardley 2012).[3] The very success of such policies at redistributing resources between different groups can, over time, result in new inequalities being the end result.

The Malaysian case reveals some interesting differences from both the United States and India. Affirmative action programmes in this country were designed to improve the economic position of the *Bumiputras*, who consisted of Malays and other indigenous peoples. These 'sons of the soil' were not in the same position as African Americans or the *dalits* in India – minority groups discriminated against and left behind in the course of social and economic development. *Bumiputras* were not only a numerical majority in the country but also enjoyed political dominance, which more nearly approximates to the situation of Africans in post-apartheid South Africa. The rest of the Malaysian population, predominantly Chinese and Indians, making up 45 per cent of the total, were economically better off than the Malays, yet were politically subordinate to the *Bumiputras*. Thus, 'the groups that received the benefits of the affirmative action policies are the ones to have the political power to legislate them' (Lim 1985: 250). This is, of course, a crucial factor and one that was a direct legacy of British colonial policies based on the 'protection' of Malay rights. The Malay ruling elites were granted symbolic sovereignty and the rest of the Malay population received certain preferences in terms of agricultural, educational and employment opportunities vis-à-vis the Chinese and Indian communities. In reality, these benefits proved to be a mixed blessing, keeping many of the Malay peasants as subsistence rice farmers while the other groups made significant advances in the industrial and commercial spheres. By 1957, at independence, only 10 per cent of registered businesses, and a mere 1.5 per cent of capital investment in them, belonged to Malays.

Decolonization resulted in a protracted bargaining process in which 'Malays who enjoyed political privilege and non-Malays who had the economic advantage . . . traded one commodity for the other' (ibid.: 256). In this manner:

> A final compromise was reached wherein non-Malays, in return for receiving citizenship based on the principle of *jus soli*, agreed to have special rights conferred on the Malays in order to uplift their economic position. Thus, Malay Special Rights were finally enshrined in Article 153 of the Federal Constitution of 1957. (ibid.)

The special rights included the reservation for *Bumiputras* of a 'reasonable proportion' of positions in the public service sector and in educational institutions, scholarships, and for trading or business permits. Under Article 89, certain areas of the country could be designated as Malay Reservation land subject to exclusive Malay ownership. Finally, these rights were so firmly entrenched that they were more difficult to amend than the Constitution itself.

Such provisions managed to generate resentment on all sides. The Malays saw little immediate result and the non-Malays disliked their increasing exclusion from educational and employment opportunities, and it was not long before these grievances resulted in the 1969 race riots. As a consequence, the laissez-faire basis of the economy made way for greater state intervention to regulate and promote Malay economic interests. Malay rights were further strengthened, and a New Economic Policy was adopted which aimed at eradicating poverty and ensuring that *Bumiputras* would achieve 30 per cent of ownership and employment by 1990. There was also a realignment of the political parties, the ethnic opposition parties being co-opted into a broad, National Front coalition. Thus, the basis for a relatively successful strategy to produce a more balanced distribution of economic resources among the major ethnic groups was set in motion. However, the rapid growth of the Malaysian economy during the next twenty-five years was a major factor in enabling this redistribution to occur with minimal friction.[4]

It was the absence of rapid economic growth that made the affirmative action policies of the first democratic South African government, despite being elected with an overwhelming ANC majority in 1994, much more difficult to implement. While few would dispute the need for a more fair distribution of economic opportunities and resources in the post-apartheid South Africa, how to achieve this goal in a relatively stagnant economy posed enormous dilemmas for the ANC government which wished to sustain the remarkable democratic transition. It is true that there was some reduction in overall racial inequality after 1994, but there has been a widening wealth gap among Africans between those with education and political connections and the under- and unemployed. The entrenched position of former government employees, guaranteed by the transitional agreement, and the lack of skills and educational qualifications among the African majority resulting from the legacy of apartheid, as well as the slow rate of economic growth, all pointed to the difficulties confronting attempts to narrow the enormous racial inequalities facing contemporary South Africa. As one acute observer noted:

> One of the greatest inherent risks of affirmative action [in South Africa] lies in nurturing the same racial divide which underpinned apartheid ... Using race-based affirmative action to benefit blacks as a group, without distinguishing between the relatively privileged stratum and those who are 'truly disadvantaged', detracts from assisting those most in need, particularly in a society in which the target groups form the numerical majority. (Adam 2000: 180)

Even more complex has been the attempted implementation of affirmative action policies in Brazil. Legislation in 2004 established a racial quota reserving 20 per cent of the positions at the elite, public University of Brasilia for black and mixed-race students. Middle- and upper-middle-class students are generally white and receive their earlier education in private schools that are far better funded and supported than the public high schools where most of the black and mixed-race students attend. One of the key problems, which is rarely encountered in other systems experimenting with affirmative action, concerns identifying those who should receive such assistance. This is because, despite a clear hierarchy based on skin colour as far as income, wealth, education and political power are concerned, families often have members with quite varied appearances. The system uses a process of visual categorization, based on colour photographs included in students' application forms, and panels assessing the eligibility of applicants for such quota positions have even ranked identical twins in different ways! Nevertheless, in April 2012, the Brazilian Supreme Court upheld the racial quota policy at the University of Brasilia and in August of the same year extended the system to all of the nation's superior and largely free public universities, in what has been called the 'Law of Social Quotas'. How effective this strategy will be in reducing inequality between Brazilians of different colours remains to be seen, but it certainly represents a dramatic retreat from the claims of 'racial democracy' that allowed denial that any race relations 'problem' existed in the country. It also forms a stark contrast between the policies in the United States, with its strong opposition to any policy couched in the language of 'quotas', and the successive narrowing by the US Supreme Court of universities' ability to take race into account when selecting students (Lipka 2013). The question of how much this difference is the result of the contrasting population ratios involved, with the implications this might have as far as group power is concerned, forms the basis of one possible suggestion, since a slight majority of Brazil's 196 million people identify as black or mixed race, while the comparable figures for the United States would be much less than 20 per cent (Ibram H. Rogers, 5 November 2012).

The problem of justice

This brief survey of a few important examples of affirmative action/preferential policies raises a series of general themes. While attempts to draw lessons out of the experience of one society to apply to another are always dangerous, since each society has unique characteristics and a distinct history, nonetheless exploring common patterns – in the Weberian tradition – can provide valuable insight. At least ten general issues are raised by our analysis.

1 *Costs, benefits and time*: One does not need to be a convinced rational choice theorist to accept that most policies involve a mix of costs and benefits. A claim made by Horowitz (1985: 653–80) in his 1985 overview of the way that preference policies impact on ethnic conflict is that the costs of such projects are experienced immediately, while the benefits tend to be delivered at a much later date. This is particularly true in the American and Indian cases, where the affirmative action is geared to redressing minority disadvantage, rather than in the Malaysian or South African situations. In democratic political systems, when the majority is likely to bear the 'cost' of such policies, the electoral backlash against them, due to this timing problem, is a major obstacle.

2 *Symbolism versus reality*: Critics of affirmative action make the point that such policies tend to be cosmetic and rarely address the fundamental problems generating inequality. The act of proposing targets or quotas in higher education or employment fails to rectify inequities in primary and secondary education, or in levels of technical skill and managerial experience. Instead of fixing the basic problems, affirmative action policies divert attention away from them and also may place under-qualified individuals in a position where they can fail to meet minimum performance standards or complete academic courses. This sets in motion a self-fulfilling prophecy and feeds the stereotypes of those opposed to greater assistance to the disadvantaged minorities in society.

3 *Individual versus group rights*: Affirmative action policies also raise potentially difficult moral questions concerning inter-generational accountability, and individual as opposed to collective responsibility. While many would accept the need to take some action to compensate for past categorical discrimination, when specific individuals are confronted with situations where they lose out to those they perceive as 'less qualified' members of other ethnic or racial groups, there is a tendency to interpret this as *reversed racism*. Pointing to the historical record, to the current legacy of unequal opportunities, or to the dubious nature of many 'objective' indices of

merit (SAT scores; IQ tests, etc.) provides little comfort to individuals on the losing end of these decisions. In political systems where such individuals are part of the democratic majority, this invites a significant electoral backlash.

4   *Class or race?*: The skewed social class impact of different types of preferential policies has been noted in many situations. Some will argue that this is not a critical issue, certainly in the early phases of redistributional strategies. To include members of formerly disadvantaged elites *can* be an essential step in reducing ethnic violence and conflict, and such leaders act as vital role models – what the sociologist and pioneering Civil Rights advocate W. E. B. DuBois called the 'Talented Tenth' – to inspire hope and emulation. However, when an increasing economic chasm opens up between the newly affluent and a dangerously alienated underclass, the time has probably arrived to recalibrate the targeting of affirmative action policies to ensure a greater focus on economic, as much as racial or ethnic, justice. William J. Wilson's concern for the 'truly disadvantaged' (1987, 1996) and the Indian Supreme Court's rulings in the 1990s reflect this realignment.

5   *The limits of action*: Whether one regards preference policies as part of the solution or part of the problem, it is still important to specify what the aims of the exercise are. It is certainly the case that affirmative action is not a panacea for solving ethnic conflicts, although it can be argued that it may be a necessary, if not a sufficient, condition for achieving a measure of long-term racial harmony. While racial and ethnic conflicts are not solely about distributional imbalances, economic and social inequities tend to exacerbate these situations.

6   *Indirect benefits*: There are a number of ways in which affirmative action policies have valuable side effects unrelated to any redistributional impact. These include pressures to expand opportunities; increasing the pool of talent; improvements in efficiency; and the encouragement of political mobilization. In the Malaysian case, for example, the expansion of private education and eventually public education, as well as the

exploitation of overseas educational opportunities, resulted from the pressures created by the Malay Rights policies. In other words, some of the indirect and longer-term benefits that came to all segments of the society included both human capital and social capital (by expanding global networks).

7 *Problems of corruption*: Some critics have maintained that attempts to radically alter economic management and ownership inevitably lead to incentives for bribery and corruption. In order to meet racial or ethnic targets, existing entrepreneurs appoint token directors and managers, a policy that simply adds to costs and brings about little structural change. The so-called 'Ali-Baba' corporations in Malaysia offer a typical example of this arrangement. While this may happen in the short run, it is necessary to evaluate the longer-term outcome of such regulations. In South Africa, Anglo-American, the giant mining company, and other major conglomerates struck deals with aspiring Nationalist businessmen after 1948, which undoubtedly enhanced Afrikaner entrepreneurial success over the next few decades. A similar accommodation took place after the 1994 democratic transition, with prominent African leaders, like the trade unionist and leading ANC member Cyril Ramaphosa, being incorporated into the South African business elite.

8 *Alternative strategies*: Several critics have suggested that public policy can be more effective in bringing about greater ethnic equality by using non-racial strategies. This is a parallel argument to the advocates of class-based affirmative action, and stresses the beneficial outcomes of regional investment and location decisions that attack ethnic inequalities in a more indirect manner. If the reduction of ethnic conflict is the paramount goal, such strategies have their merits, although care must be taken not to foster a sense of regional resentment in the process.

9 *Affirmative action for whom?*: In multi-racial and multi-ethnic societies, another major issue arises as to which groups should be eligible for preferential treatment. In America, opinions differ on whether affirmative action ought to be

confined to African Americans and Native Americans, or whether Latinos, Asian Americans and women should also be included. Moskos and Butler (1996) in their study of the American military argued that blacks should be the only recipients of preference policies; others strongly disagree. The legitimate scope of affirmative action is clearly an important and complex question that has affected most societies engaging in these policies; the United States and South Africa have faced similar questions on this issue.

10 *Avoiding a zero-sum game:* A particularly vital factor, as all our case studies suggest, is the economic context in which these policies are pursued. Other things being equal, the faster the rate of economic growth of the total economy, the less disruptive will be the process of resource redistribution that lies at the heart of the affirmative action strategy. Much of the success of the Malaysian situation, which at the outset – in the aftermath of the deadly 1969 race riots – was full of potential conflict, can be attributed to the rapid and sustained expansion of the economy. In the two decades following the democratic transition in South Africa, no such rapid growth in the wealth of the country took place, which made the successful implementation of redistribution more difficult. However, strong opposition to affirmative action in the United States in the decades prior to the Great Recession of 2008 took place during a period of sustained economic expansion, but the crucial difference is that the benefits of this extra wealth were confined to an increasingly small segment of society – the very wealthy. It was only after the recession had persisted for two to three years that resentment about redistribution started to include the top-income earners, not just racial and ethnic minorities, as articulated by the Occupy Wall Street movement. Nevertheless, right-wing populist groups such as the Tea Party (Skocpol and Williamson 2012) focused their discontent on 'big government' interference in the everyday lives of citizens, but their overwhelming white membership continued opposition to policies designed to rectify minority disadvantage.

The conservative response to the goal of reducing racial and ethnic inequality has focused on colour-blind measures to create more opportunity for all.[5] Such programmes usually include plans to: (i) establish renewal communities and enterprise zones to draw business and jobs into distressed urban areas; (ii) open up the educational system to the influence of parental and community choice; (iii) reverse federal and state welfare provisions to reward rather than punish recipients for working, saving and investing towards an independent future; (iv) implement privatization of public housing and other efforts to bring home ownership and property ownership into low-income neighbourhoods; and (v) generally encourage faster economic growth that will include all groups in American society. While many, particularly in the light of the 2008 Wall Street crash, might question the efficacy of this market-driven strategy, these measures attempt to respond to William J. Wilson's focus on the lack of employment in America's inner cities as a critical factor in creating an urban underclass. Citing Frederick Douglass's remark to fellow African Americans in the nineteenth century, 'when we are noted for enterprise, industry and success, we shall no longer have any trouble in the matter of civil and political rights', Wilson's position makes a powerful case for strengthening the economic base of the black community, but the matter in dispute concerns what mixture of economic and political forces are needed to achieve this goal. Weber, no doubt, would have regarded the economic and the political – economy and society – as inseparable components of group position and power, concluding that no invisible hand can achieve a successful outcome without the use of both economic and political forces.

The perils of prediction

These twentieth-century changes in the global power structure, particularly from the 1960s onwards, resulted in a very different set of questions and priorities being addressed by social scientists. This is particularly true of issues linked to the nature of racial conflict. How many of the older conflicts have remained and how many have changed in directions that were not anticipated in previous decades? What is the nature of the new forms of group definition and boundary conflicts, and what are the chances that these will be exacerbated or diminished by the forces unleashed by a post-ideological age? While the capitalist consensus has spread from Shanghai to Sofia and from Mumbai to Mexico City, in what manner will this new pattern of global materialism interact with the emerging movements of nationalism and religious fundamentalism that have resurfaced as serious political forces in the United States, the Middle East and Africa? The same question also applies to the immigrant and minority communities in Europe, not to mention the minority groups and diaspora communities found in other parts of the world.

Such basic questions set the broad context for so many of the current debates in the field of race and ethnic relations. If we look back several decades to the end of the 1980s, prominent issues at that time consisted of a range of racial and ethnic conflicts. The Israeli–Palestinian struggle continued in the Middle East; Northern Ireland and the Basque country remained enduring areas of conflict in Western Europe; Kashmir and Sri Lanka were regions of violence in South Asia; in Central America states like Nicaragua and Guatemala displayed the levels of human destruction characteristic of bitter civil wars; while the unravelling of the colonial legacy in Africa generated a number of vicious ethnic struggles. However, perhaps the most salient focus of international concern in the last region was on the developing events in apartheid South Africa, a particularly important conflict since the subsequent outcome was almost entirely unexpected. Yet another part of the world that had historically been noted for its complex inter-group tensions – so much so that the region had given birth to a specific term, *Balkanization*, to describe such intricate patterns of national, linguistic, religious and ethnic conflicts (Rizova 2006) – seemed, in the 1980s, to be a rather unlikely candidate for savage warfare and what became known subsequently as 'ethnic cleansing' (Sekulić et al. 2006). Examining these contrasting cases of conflict resolution and conflict generation can provide some clues to the shifting dynamic of inter-group relations in the immediate post-Cold War era.

While most outside observers recognized that the apartheid regime was inherently unstable, few predicted that the development of racial conflict in South Africa would be resolved in the manner that it was.[6] Sociologists and political scientists, in general, saw the superimposition of race on class divisions as leading to the polarization of the society in a form that would not easily result in a compromise between the various racial and ethnic components of the apartheid state. Cross-cutting cleavages are often seen as the sociopolitical mechanism which leads to the mediation of conflicts and the prevention of structural faults, in deeply divided social systems, which can help to inoculate them from breaking apart into communal violence. The very nature and the dynamics of the apartheid system were designed to stop such ameliorating networks from developing, and to destroy even those that had naturally occurred despite all the customary hostility and state restrictions, by a reclassification of individuals into mutually exclusive groups. In this way, by reinforcing group boundaries and undermining inter-group associations, any serious hope of moderation and compromise appeared to have been banished from the system.

The actual outcome, at the time, seemed extremely unlikely and few observers expected that the small white elite would have the insight or ability to negotiate a transfer of power to the African majority. Equally implausible was the proposition that the African population and its leaders, representing more than 75 per cent of the total population and after years of dispossession and crude exploitation, would be prepared to accept such a deal, without a simultaneous and radical redistribution of economic resources. Explaining the nature of the South African transition is a particular challenge as it defies many of the most influential theories of revolutionary political action – the concept of *relative deprivation* and the associated phenomenon of the *revolution of rising expectations* that we have described earlier. None of these much-quoted social psychological mechanisms – that can be traced back at least as far as Alexis de Tocqueville's writings in the middle of the nineteenth century (Tocqueville 1856; Stone and Mennell 1980) – seemed as if they would play a major role in the demise of apartheid. However, the South African experience of negotiated regime change moved the country from being an archetypal illustration of conflict generation to the favourite case study of those involved in the emerging discipline of conflict resolution.[7]

A number of factors were recognized, retrospectively, to be particularly critical in bringing about this implausibly benign outcome. First, the end of the Cold War, resulting from the collapse of the Soviet Union in 1989, and the many proxy wars that were sustained by this ideological rivalry which caused such chaos throughout large sectors of sub-Saharan Africa, was one of the most important forces which shifted the internal balance of power in an important new direction. A second element in the reappraisal of the dynamics of the democratic transition was an increasing appreciation of the political skills and social acumen displayed by many of the leaders of the anti-apartheid struggle. Whether social and political scientists emphasize or play down the role of agency, as opposed to structural factors, in being the prime cause of political change seems to be as variable as the shifts in theoretical fashion. Most analysts recognize that the murderous legacy of Hitler, Stalin or Mao, in understanding the Holocaust, the Gulags and the Cultural Revolution, or, on a numerically smaller but similarly brutal scale, the activities of Pol Pot in Cambodia, should not be left out of the explanation. However, the constructive role of enlightened leadership is often under-appreciated by scholars, perhaps as a reaction to the personality cults of the tyrants of history.

It is true that Gandhi's non-violent campaign to achieve independence in India was slightly tarnished by his failure to preserve unity between Hindus and Muslims at the time of partition (Parekh 1997). Furthermore, the glaring contrast between the 'success' of Gandhi's non-violent tactics in India, and their comprehensive failure in South Africa just a few decades earlier, suggests that the charisma of an individual is not a necessary, let alone a sufficient, cause to explain the outcome of most cases of political mobilization. However, few would totally discount the personal qualities – Weber's *charisma* – that sustained Mandela's crusade against apartheid over a period of some three decades. The unusual political skills that enabled this exceptional individual to consolidate the power of the African majority, while undermining resistance to change among the white minority, is almost certainly one of the most important independent factors that led to the relatively peaceful conclusion to this particular inter-racial struggle. If Mandela and his comrades had been executed after the Rivonia trial in 1963 and 1964, would this macro-level struggle and outcome have been essentially the same in 1994? While we can never know for sure the answer to this question, most observers and participants in these events would not dismiss the importance of skilful and far-sighted leadership. This was also the assessment of Archbishop Desmond Tutu, another South African awarded the Nobel Peace Prize and a central figure in the Truth and Reconciliation Commission set up to manage the post-apartheid transition, who declared at the time of Mandela's death, 'If this man wasn't there, the country would have gone up in flames' (Feeney 2013)

A third factor that supported the profound pessimism of most observers of the South African situation was a failure to adequately recognize the generational shifts in both the leadership and support base of the minority-controlled elite. In many respects, apartheid was becoming unnecessary, an outmoded and counterproductive strategy for an increasingly affluent and well-educated Afrikaner community. As the *bywoners*, the poor whites, prospered and faced extinction as a category – thus no longer representing the crucial power bloc that had elevated the National Party to control of the South African parliament in 1948 – security and competitive strength reduced the need for crude racial separation. Increasingly, a growing number of Afrikaners moved towards the position of the more moderate section of the English-speaking white elite, in wishing to avoid the costs associated with the global sanctions that apartheid had generated, having made full use of affirmative action to enhance their wealth and income during four decades of uninterrupted power. The prospect of losing the tacit support of their Cold War allies, the serious enforcement of trade and financial sanctions, and the cost–benefit assessment between the carrot of an open Southern African economic market as against the stick of increasing military incursions and local opposition, further tipped the scales in favour of serious negotiation. While the outcome was never inevitable, the South African case points to the need to carefully evaluate a wide range of internal and external factors, and their interaction and change over time, before reaching any conclusions about the probable direction of race and ethnic relations.

The 'success' of South Africa needs to be set against the 'failure' of Yugoslavia to contain its ethnic and national diversity in the transition to multi-party democracy during the post-communist period. Given the history of the region, and the creation of Yugoslavia as a multinational state in the wake of the collapse of the Ottoman and Austro-Hungarian empires in 1919, few scholars and outside observers would have expected the future of Yugoslavia to be without problems. However, when looking at the wide range of states affected by the demise of the Soviet domination in Eastern Europe and the Russian periphery, only Chechnya proved to be an arena of comparable violent conflict.

In many respects, the former Yugoslavia appeared to be one of the less likely areas destined for destructive dissolution as a result of a much-diminished oppressive regime prior to the post-communist era. It also had a decentralized federal system that permitted a considerable measure of autonomy in its ethnically diverse regions, a higher level of economic achievement and a greater number of contacts through tourism and links to the more open institutions of Western Europe. None of this, however, was able to staunch the resurgence of bitter nationalism that was manipulated by members of the former political elites in a bid to reassert control over the total territory – in the case of the Serbs – or to break away and consolidate power within independent states dominated by the majority ethnic group, as in the cases of Slovenia, Croatia and Bosnia-Herzegovina. While in the aftermath of the dissolution of Yugoslavia scholars were able to explain the dynamic processes that had contributed to this bloody outcome, the most convincing analyses benefited considerably from hindsight. Recognizing the changing balances of power in the post-Cold War realignments, and seeing how these were likely to impact the internal relations, provided a clearer understanding of why the various communities, and particularly their leaders, took the path towards warfare, separation and ethnic cleansing, rather than trying to resolve their differences by compromise and discussion. The interest that the Slovenian and Croatian elites had in joining with the Serbs in the second decade of the twentieth century had been sustained during the Cold War, but it rapidly diminished in the post-communist period. At this point, the former leaders preferred the prospect of joining an expanding European Union, while those comprising the old communist power structure – albeit now regrouped under nationalist ideology – did not. As Duško Sekulić concluded: 'A bipolar world held Yugoslavia together as a result of pressures from both sides; the disappearance of bi-polarity meant the collapse of the outside forces keeping Yugoslavia intact' (1997: 177).

The contrasting developments in South Africa and Yugoslavia, taking place at much the same time, but on different continents and with diametrically opposite results, have one thing in common. In both cases, the outcome of group conflicts did not follow a path that most academic experts expected. It is a cautionary tale that is a useful prelude to considering the types of trends that will most likely affect the patterns of race and ethnic relations and the probability of racial conflict in the future. Furthermore, it highlights the need to consider the complexities of power and its relationship to group conflict, a theme that reinforces the wisdom of a multi-causal, Weberian perspective.

The debate with the ghost of Weber

In the preceding chapters, we have examined the interplay between power, conflict and race relations in all their complexity in the modern world. We have selectively illustrated the diverse patterns found in different societies during various historical eras and attempted to show that while each situation has certain unique characteristics, nevertheless it is possible to discover common features in most cases of racial conflict and racial stratification. As a guiding theme we have used a modified version of our interpretation of Weber's preliminary model of social group formation and boundary maintenance, suitably adapted to incorporate the relations between members of diverse racial, ethnic and national groups. It is true that not all Weberian scholars share the same perspective on how to employ his seminal writings to this field. Prominent social scientists have made a case that Weber's later, unfinished musings on these topics point to a rather different focus that might be derived from his earlier writings on the subject (Banton 2014; see also Brubaker 2013). This perspective joins with the approaches found particularly in economics and political science that argue for a more 'methodological individualist' perspective on human behaviour and seek to demonstrate that too much scholarship in this field exaggerates the extent to which collective features of society – ethnic and racial groups, cultures, identities etc. – can be used to understand what is taking place in situations of racial conflict.[8]

We would agree with such scholars, and with certain strands in Weber's methodological thinking, that individuals do play a central role in social life that should not be ignored. However, just as criticisms of 'essentialism' are well taken – not all members of a particular racial or ethnic group think or behave in a certain fashion, no matter how strong a 'master' identity might appear to over-rule most other possible forms of allegiance – similarly attempts to 'reduce' group conflicts to individual 'tastes and preferences' are equally distorted. Ultimately, social life is a complex interplay between collective and individual forces and any analysis that tries to ignore one at the expense of the other is bound to be one-sided. It is our view that Weber's struggle to resolve this methodological dilemma can be seen in the contrast between much of his actual writings, brilliant attempts to explain the shape of the modern world, and his more formal methodological perspective that attempts to incorporate individual perceptions and values into the analysis. Just as Murphy (1988) has argued for a hierarchy of boundary mechanisms, rather than the more random, historical and chance explanation of racial and ethnic group formation, so we would argue that in the field of racial conflict collective forces in the situation often, though not always, tend to predominate over individualistic features of the interaction. In no sense does this dismiss the role of charismatic leaders – such as Mahatma Gandhi, Martin Luther King or Nelson Mandela – in helping to shift the outcome of race relations in a manner contrary to what one would superficially see as overwhelming power imbalances. Nor does it diminish the role of thousands of less well-known figures whose courage and selfless determination have helped to upset systems of brutal exploitation and savage oppression.

Nevertheless, for long periods of time the collective balance of power has tended to sustain and resist change to all manner of exploitative systems of racial oppression, whether they involve racial slavery, apartheid, caste divisions or Jim Crow segregation and violence. Change does take place; no human institutions or even deeply entrenched cultural values remain static for ever, and the role of individual actions in promoting such change, often through a process of collective mobilization, is critical. However, we need to be careful to avoid falling into the evolutionary assumptions that are implicit in so many theories of social change throughout the nineteenth and twentieth centuries. Thus Norbert Elias, to take just one example, could publish his monumental work on *The Civilizing Process* in German during 1939, six years after escaping to France and then to England to avoid the Nazi menace.[9] Elias, a distinguished German-Jewish sociologist, fleeing persecution and, as was revealed subsequently, the systematic murder of some 6 million European Jews in the gas chambers, appeared to be preoccupied with what he saw as the developmental growth of 'civilization', such as table manners and courtly habits, just as his own society was collapsing into barbarism.

In a later variation on a similar theme, the evolutionary psychologist Steven Pinker has suggested in *The Better Angels of Our Nature: Why Violence Has Declined* (2011) an analogous position that has very little empirical data to support it. While it is extremely difficult to measure levels of violence, particularly when analysing complex settings of racial and ethnic conflict, there seems to be as little evidence to support Pinker's claims about contemporary society as there were for Elias's perspective in the 1930s. One is reminded of Gandhi's response when asked by a reporter for his thoughts on 'Western civilization' – 'I think it would be a nice idea'. Even among prominent scholars, the power of ethnocentric assumptions can so often blind them to what an outsider would regard as self-evident truth.

What we have attempted to demonstrate in the preceding chapters is the extent to which racial, ethnic and national conflicts fall into familiar patterns of social stratification linked to the differential access to power in societies throughout the world. While fundamental shifts in the geo-political structure of twenty-first-century global society suggest that former hierarchies will continue to crumble and new types of boundaries and sources of identity will be created, there is no necessary path towards the end of such conflicts. Global organizations and corporations that span different continents, with diverse leaders and workforces, create new challenges that reflect the underlying changes that we have been describing. Whether new institutions will be able to shape the direction of social life in a more constructive and cooperative direction during the twenty-first century remains an open question. One thing, however, is certain: without a sense of justice,[10] cultural sensitivity and an understanding of the true complexity of modern society, the prospect of reducing future racial conflict will be little better than it has been in the past.

This somewhat pessimistic conclusion, very much in line with Weber's own concerns about the future shape of modern society – the 'iron cage' brought about by the relentless pursuit of rationality in the form of increasing, impersonal bureaucracy, combined with his political realism – is but one interpretation of how power and racial conflict are aligned. Others may take a more hopeful position, and view a longer perspective on race and ethnic relations, showing how the determined behaviour of human actors has managed to overcome entrenched power structures and challenged the domination of particular racial, ethnic and national groups. The fiftieth anniversary celebrations of the March on Washington and Martin Luther King's 'I have a Dream' speech in August 1963 perhaps present a more sober assessment of these issues in the United States in the summer of 2013. On the one hand, the reality of the end of legalized segregation, of an African-American President and Attorney General, and a substantial black middle class, must be set against persistent racial inequalities in education, housing and wealth. Furthermore, the Supreme Court's decision to gut the 1965 Voting Rights Act and the controversial jury verdict in the Trayvon Martin killing suggest that while much has been achieved, the price of liberty remains eternal vigilance. Finally, what is true for the United States also remains the case for a global society increasingly diverse in its racial and ethnic composition and more closely integrated by technological change and international migration.

Notes

Chapter 1. Diversity: Conflicts in the New Millennium

1 The original BRIC group was expanded in 2010 to include South Africa. A further collection of emergent economies, using the acronym MIST – Mexico, Indonesia, South Korea and Turkey – provides the latest signs of rapid economic growth in societies with highly diverse ethnic, racial and religious compositions (Martin 2012).

2 A related argument can be seen in Bonilla-Silva's notion of a 'racial grammar' blinding many whites in America from a clear appreciation of racial injustice. See Eduardo Bonilla-Silva (2012) – the 'whiteness' debate, 'The invisible weight of whiteness: The racial grammar of everyday life in contemporary America', *Ethnic and Racial Studies* 35/2: 173–94. This is also related to the discussion about the difficulty of many in the white majority to understand the structural biases faced by minorities of colour. It is further linked to the debates about 'identity politics', 'multiculturalism' and similar issues explored in greater detail in chapter 6.

3 For an exploration of these complicated questions, see Jeremy Waldron (2012), *The Harm in Hate Speech*.

4 The clash between Tocqueville and Gobineau, after the release of the latter's *Inequality of the Human Races*, also saw the former using evidence from the Roman Empire to demolish racial theorizing. For further details about the uneasy friendship between the two, see Hugh Brogan (2006: 545–6, 592–5).

5 For a discussion of 'reflexivity', see Bonilla-Silva's articles in *Ethnic and Racial Studies* (2012).

6 See Anthony Smith's (1992) discussion of the survival of ethnic groups, 'Chosen Peoples: Why Ethnic Groups Survive', *Ethnic and Racial Studies* 15: 436–56. See also his more extended discussion of the same issues in *Chosen Peoples: Sacred Sources of National Identity* (Oxford: Oxford University Press, 2003).

7 No better illustration of this can be found in Henry Louis Gates's PBS documentaries, *African American Lives*, looking at the probable ancestry of prominent African-American celebrities as revealed by genetic testing. *Presumed* ancestry is the key here. For some, sociobiology still provides a bridge between actual ancestry and group solidarity. It is interesting that some thinkers, no matter how much the biological or genetic theories have been dismissed by overwhelming evidence, seem to be attracted back to this level of analysis. This is not in any sense suggesting that such thinkers are 'racist'; quite clearly many have been prominent public critics of racism – Pierre van den Berghe, for example. But the seductive allure of some deterministic paradigm that claims to explain the fundamental 'laws' of group behaviour – the genetic selfishness of social insects like ants and bees as described by E. O. Wilson – and that can be transposed on to human beings, becomes overwhelming. What are the genetic advantages of celibate priesthoods; or that more murders take place within families than among strangers; or the entirely altruistic acts of those that lay down their lives to help total strangers? (Casiro 2010). These common social facts suggest that sociobiological perspectives are an over-simplistic and reductionist explanation of human behaviour.

8 For comparable examples of attitude change, see the case of British migrants to apartheid South Africa in the 1960s (Stone, *Colonist or Uitlander*, 1973), and the responses to stigmatization in comparative perspectives, Lamont and Mizrachi (eds), in *Ethnic and Racial Studies* 35/3 (March 2012).

9 Only the libertarians, on the far right of the political spectrum, with their advocacy of open borders, hold a consistent position on the issue of immigration. Ron Paul – dismissed by many as a crank – seemed to support such a strategy in his 2012 presidential bid. Equally, left-wing political parties, given their strong backing from the trade union movement, are similarly suspicious of the free flow of workers from overseas. To them, such policies benefit business interests by reducing wages and can be seen as the other face of 'outsourcing'.

10 The additional twist that more recent events have given to these debates is the question concerning the viability of some of the many smaller states – Somalia and Mali being prime examples of 'failed' or 'almost failed' states – in a world increasingly dominated by multinational conglomerates, and the new threats to both these and more established and powerful states resulting from the pressures generated by non-state actors like global terrorist networks. Pablo Escobar, the Colombian drug lord, was the leader of the Medellin cartel until he was killed in 1993, and was reputed at that time to be among the ten richest men in the world according to *Fortune* and *Forbes* magazines. The authority of dominant world powers has frequently been challenged by a variety of 'predators and parasites' – drug traffickers, mercenaries, pirates and terrorists – when indeed the decision not to co-opt

such non-state actors has been made by these same powers as a means of serving their own ends (Lowenheim 2006). After all, Lord Palmerston, the architect of Britain's 'opium wars' against China during the mid-nineteenth century, could be regarded as acting in a rather similar manner to such notorious, twentieth-century drug lords as Pablo Escobar, but the British prime minister was an even more dangerous individual as he controlled a military superpower. However, every non-state actor need not be seen as necessarily destructive or evil, as global environmental, medical and human rights organizations often act as counter-weights to the short-sighted policies of particular states, corporations or other global alliances of the powerful. Unfortunately, the power to do good, as opposed to the power to commit evil, is often asymmetrical, so that these positive forces are frequently left to try to mitigate the negative consequences of destructive social actors, as Kofi Annan's vain attempt to promote peaceful conflict resolution in Syria during the 2012 uprising against the Assad regime clearly demonstrated (*Boston Globe*, 3 August 2012, A3).

11 One of the most careful critiques of Weber's unfinished writings on ethnic groups can be found in Michael Banton's work. Unlike our position that sees little contradiction between the collective concepts of ethnic, 'racial' or national groups, and the behaviour and responses of individual actors – two different, but ultimately inseparable, perspectives on the same issue of 'the one and the many' – Banton argues that Weber himself was left with an irreconcilable dilemma. This is not surprising given Banton's attraction to rational choice theories. However, he does make the interesting point that 'for the study of ethnic relations, and particularly for consideration of social integration, analysis of how people come to leave groups is at least as important as analysis of what brought them into the groups in the first place' (see Banton 2007: 27–8) and his forthcoming article in *The Journal of Classical Sociology* (2014), available online as of 1 August 2013).

Chapter 2. Power: The Changing Geo-politics of Race

1 For an interesting, if somewhat ironic, variant on the idea of 'false consciousness', see the collaboration of Western media and high-tech companies with the restrictions imposed by the Communist Party leadership on the free flow of ideas within China, e.g., 'Google in China: Search No Evil', at: <http://www.theguardian.com/technology/blog/2006/jan/28/googleinchina>.

2 Thomas M. Shapiro (2004) uses the concept of 'opportunity hoarding' – passing on assets between generations – which favours whites over blacks at a ratio of 10:1. See also Ira Katznelson (2006), who links white 'affirmative action' to the New Deal and to policies to assist white veterans, notably the GI Bill after the Second World War. The idea that apartheid in South Africa, between 1948 and 1990, was another form of affirmative action for the domi-

nant (white) political group, and its demonstrated effectiveness in raising the lower classes of Afrikaners – the *bywoners* – out of poverty, is a similar argument (Stone and Rizova 2007: 537). And for yet another illustration of the same theme – preferential treatment for the children of wealthy white alumni and donors to American elite Universities – see Peter Schmidt (2007).

3 See the figures quoted in the *Boston Globe* (23 September 2007). The annual cost of maintaining America's correctional institutions is $60 billion with approximately 2.2 million inmates comprising the prison population. Of black males born in the late 1960s who did not attend college, 30 per cent have served time in prison, while 59 per cent of the same cohort who did not finish high school have also served time in prison.

4 In March 2007, an amendment to the Cherokee Constitution to limit citizenship to 'those who are Indian "by blood"' was approved by 77 per cent of Cherokee voters. The Freedmen, descendants of former slaves owned by the Cherokee, represent barely 1 per cent of the tribe. A similar vote by the Seminole nation in 2000 was subsequently overturned when the Federal government cut off funds to the tribe and the decision was successfully challenged in Federal Court.

5 According to Winant's assessment: 'In the racial future, I venture to predict, there will be a combination of greater flexibility in the understanding of racial identity on the one hand, and a deepening structural racism on the other. That is to say the global racial crisis will intensify, not diminish' (2006: 999). This is not unlike Bonilla-Silva's prediction of the growing 'Latin Americanization' of the United States (2006: 183–98).

6 For further exploration of these issues, see Jennifer Lee and Frank Bean, *The Diversity Paradox*: *Immigration and the Colour Line in Twenty-First Century America* (2010).

7 Perhaps the best use of the historical evidence to demolish racial theorizing can be found in Alexis de Tocqueville's response to the central theme of Arthur de Gobineau's influential book *On the Inequality of the Human Races* (1856) (Stone 1977: 62; Stone and Mennell 1980: 320–2).

8 On Darfur, Prunier describes the situation as a 'complex ethnic mosaic', rightly pointing out that the diversity is not confined to the differences between 'Arabs' and 'Africans', but also different linguistic variations that cut across this dichotomy, not to mention other group boundaries, so that 'In terms of skin colour everyone is black. But the various forms of Sudanese cultural racism distinguish "zurug" from "Arab" even if the skin has the same colour' (2005: 4) – another illustration of 'colour-blind racism'!

Chapter 3. Boundaries: Identity in the New World Disorder

1 We borrow this term from Kevin Avruch's perceptive and witty essay, 'Culture and Ethnic Conflict in the New World Disorder', in Stone and

Dennis (2003: 72–82). For his subsequent thoughts on related issues, see his provocative ideas in Kevin Avruch, *Context and Pretext in Conflict Resolution: Culture, Identity, Power and Practice* (2012).

2 For those who did go to the colonies, attitudes rapidly changed and writers as different as James Bryce and Frederick Engels noted the impact of the colonial experience. See John Stone, *Colonist or Uitlander?* (1973: 91–145).

3 Yet another reversal took place after the Great Recession of 2008, with youth migration from Southern Europe, particularly Greece, Spain, Italy and Portugal, and Ireland to Northern Europe, North America and Latin America, in search of employment.

4 The 2012 re-election of Barack Obama for a second term as president was achieved with the overwhelming support of Latino voters, and what was particularly crucial was their role in the 10–12 'swing states' that determined the outcome of the 'Electoral College'. This has resulted in a fundamental change in the discourse on 'immigration reform', strengthening the Democrats' will to address the problem of providing a path to citizenship for the 12 million undocumented (illegal) migrants in the country, and has even convinced most Republicans that opposing such reforms could be political suicide for the party. The demographic shifts in the composition of the electorate clearly pose an escalating threat to any political party that alienates minority voters.

5 Beth Roy's analysis of 'Rioting Across Continental Divides' (2003: 191–207) is an earlier illustration of the manner in which shifting political boundaries can impact inter-group relationships. In her case, the focus is on a community whose location 'changed' from being part of India before 1947, then came under the control of the independent Pakistani state, but subsequently, following the secession of East Pakistan to form Bangladesh in 1971, arrived at yet another geo-political environment. The violence and bloodshed associated with the successive struggles for independence, and the changing power structures linked to them, pose major problems for the various ethnic groups involved.

6 For more details on the similarities and differences between the European and American colonial experiences, see Go (2008, 2011).

7 While Obama's origins are highly diverse, the child of a Kenyan father and a white mother from Kansas, who spent much of his childhood in Indonesia and Hawaii, it is a measure of the American traditional system of racial categorization – the one-drop rule – that he is generally regarded as African American. There have, of course, been those who, for various reasons, have disputed this categorization.

8 For further exploration of these issues, see Jennifer Lee and Frank Bean, *The Diversity Paradox: Immigration and the Colour Line in Twenty-First Century America* (2010).

9 Annual Report of the Urban League, *Redeem the Dream: Jobs Rebuild America* (National Urban League 2013). At: <http://iamempowered.com/node/74570>.

10　Stacey Anderson, 'Black People Still Face Inequality' (Associated Press, 11 April 2013).

11　*The End of the Segregated Century* (Glaeser and Vigdor 2012).

12　Sam Roberts, *New York Times* (31 January 2012).

13　Annie Lowrey, 'Wealth Gap Between Whites, Minorities Widening', *New York Times* (29 April 2013); Signe-Mary McKernan, Caroline Ratcliffe, C. Eugene Steuer and Sisi Zhang, Urban Institute Report, *Less than Equal: Racial Disparities in Wealth Accumulation* (26 April 2013). At: <http://www.urban.org/UploadedPDF/412802-Less-Than-Equal-Racial-Disparities-in-Wealth-Accumulation.pdf>.

14　*Failure to Launch: Structural Shift and the New Lost Generation.* Center on Education and the Workforce Report: Georgetown University Center on Education and the Workforce, Jeff Strohl and Anthony P. Carnevale (August 2013).

15　Michael A. Fletcher, 'College Students Take Racially Separate Paths, Study Says', *Washington Post* (1 August 2013)

16　Jon Cohen and Dan Balz (2013) 'Zimmerman Verdict Poll Finds Chasm between White and Black Reactions', *Washington Post* (22 July 2013).

17　There are interesting parallels with Prohibition that are frequently overlooked as well as the extraordinary circumstances needed to pass fundamental changes in policy, and the equally dramatic pressures needed to repeal them, in the American system of check and balances and decentralized power. As Stephen Mennell observed, 'Just as the 18th Amendment (largely banning alcohol manufacture and distribution) would probably not have been carried had it not been for the First World War, so the 21st Amendment (overturning it) owed much to the Depression' (Mennell 1969: 175). For a full account, see Mennell (1969).

18　It is noteworthy that during the 2008 presidential campaign, Senator John McCain, the Republican candidate, who was born outside the United States in the Panama Canal zone, was not subjected to any questions about being a 'native-born American', unlike Senator Obama who was born in Hawaii. McCain, of course, was white.

Chapter 4. Organizations: Challenges Facing Global Institutions

1　Steven Vallas (2012) defines hyper-mobility as 'the ability of business establishments to relocate production wherever an advantageous locale could be found' (p. 140). See, also, the earlier writings of Anthony Richmond on 'transilients' and related aspects of post-industrialism, post-modernism and ethnic conflict in Stone and Dennis (eds) (2003: 83–94).

2　A further account of the unique leadership, structure and culture of the organization is offered by Manz, Shipper and Stewart (2009), '*Everyone a Team Leader: Shared Influence at W.L. Gore & Associates.*'

3 For a detailed account of the twenty-five years of trials and tribulations in the transformation process, see Semler's account in his book *Maverick: The Success Story Behind the World's Most Unusual Workplace* (1993).
4 See also Sonali Jain (2011), 'The Rights of "Return": Ethnic Identities in the Workplace among Second Generation Indian American Professionals in the Parental Homeland'.
5 Data come from <http://www.census.gov/2010census/data/>.
6 Richard Alba has developed a rather optimistic view of the impact of demographic changes on ethnic relations in the US in his recent book, *Blurring the Color Line: The New Chance for an Integrated America* (Cambridge, MA: Harvard University Press, 2009).
7 In addition to those, the Department of Homeland Security's Office of Immigration Statistics (OIS) estimates that, in 2011, 11.5 million unauthorized immigrants resided in the United States. According to the same data source, the percentage of unauthorized population has remained virtually unchanged compared to 2010, which is largely explained by the 2007–8 economic crisis.
8 Data source: <http://www.migrationpolicy.org/article/frequently-requested-statistics-immigrants-and-immigration-united-states-1>.
9 Bureau of Labor Statistics, United States Department of Labor, The Editor's Desk, 'Racial and Ethnic Characteristics of the US Labor Force, 2011'. At: <http://www.bls.gov/opub/ted/2012/ted_20120905.htm>.
10 As the previous research on social networks has demonstrated, these are merely ideal types. Universalistic criteria may be the mantra of Western business and management schools but the reality often takes a decidedly particularistic turn here as well.

Chapter 5. Violence: Extreme Racial Conflict

1 A *Symposium on War and Modernization Theory* appeared in the December 1999 issue of *International Sociology*. Responding to Hans Joas's initial article on 'The Modernity of War: Modernization Theory and the Problem of Violence', both Edward Tiryakian and Ian Roxborough provide additional ideas about how war can be better integrated into a sociological perspective. Here, the former stresses the manner in which modern warfare may be seen as a process of mobilization supporting a powerful social movement, while the latter demonstrates a number of factors – cognitive frameworks, organizational decision-making and cartelized political systems – making war quite likely in the modern world.
2 Since most of Comte's ideas concerning the fledgling discipline of sociology were greatly influenced by the ideas of Saint-Simon – 'Auguste Comte was a Saint-Simon who had been to the Ecole Polytechnique' – this is a little strange. Not only had the senior of the two thinkers been personally involved

in fighting for the Americans at the Battle of Yorktown (1781), but he had also participated in the French Revolution later in the decade. However, it was the desire to move beyond such violence to create a new harmonious society that became the obsession of both men. Saint-Simon even devised an elaborate plan to unify Western Europe, in October 1814, which might be seen as the precursor of the European Union. It took a further 150 years and two more catastrophic European wars before this became a viable project.

3 It is true that Tocqueville's travelling companion and close friend, Gustave de Beaumont, did pay greater attention to the subject of American race relations and even wrote a novel, *Marie, or, Slavery in the United States* (1835) on the subject. The aim of the work was to explore 'the violence of the prejudice which separates the race of slaves from that of free men, that is the Negroes from the whites'.

4 See Levin and Stone, 'Nationalism, Racism and the Marxist Question' (1985: 1–18).

5 The fate of the Tasmanians being one such case of the total annihilation of a whole people.

6 The classic formulation of this approach is Kuhn's work on paradigms (1962).

7 For the wider issue exploring the factors behind the interplay between democracy and despotism in much of Latin America, see Eastwood and Stone (2007).

8 The elaboration of the distinction between 'hard' and 'soft' power, reflecting the earlier distinctions emphasized by Steven Lukes, is associated with the writings of Joseph Nye (2004, 2011).

9 It is particularly surprising that the Blair government, given Britain's experience of military intervention in Belfast in the 1970s and its active involvement in peace-making in Northern Ireland, would not have anticipated this reaction in Iraq. The welcome initially extended by the subordinate group to external troops in a religiously divided community, the Catholic community to the British Army, rapidly degenerated into hostility once they were perceived as being part of the dominant (oppressive) political regime. See, also, the related and relevant arguments made by Andrew Bacevich (2008) in his critique of the Iraq and Afghanistan Wars. On the complexities of the latter society, see Thomas Barfield (2010).

10 Describing the contrasting styles of the 'practitioners of violence', Mann cites a number of sources. 'They had a style and swagger drawn from Hollywood movies. Karadzic's own daughter, stylishly dressed and sporting a Beretta pistol ("as important to me as my make-up"), said, "we got our battle ethics from the movies about Mad Max and Terminator, Rambo and Young Guns" . . . A journalist noted that in one Croat unit "everyone looks as if he had been cast as a thug by a movie director"' (Mann 2005: 419).

11 For a recent attempt to explain the Swiss situation, see Andreas Wimmer (2011).

12 The changing Turkish position represents another illustration of the impact of changes in the balances of economic and political power. For several decades, Turkey has made strong efforts to join the EU, while many European states and vocal segments of their citizens have viewed the incorporation of a Muslim society with a population the size of Germany as an existential threat to 'Christian' Europe. Since the Euro crisis following the financial collapse of 2008, together with the rapid growth of the Turkish economy, attitudes in Europe and Turkey appear to be changing in significant respects. See Gerhards and Hans (2011); Jolly and Oktay (2012).

13 For the slow growth of international institutions and law on matters of race relations since the end of the Second World War, see Michael Banton (2002).

14 See, particularly, the essays by Anthony Smith, Donald Horowitz and Joshua Fishman in Daniele Conversi (ed.) (2002: 53–90). This is one possible answer to the questions raised by Conversi: 'Does nationalism reinforce globalization or can it rather represent a challenge to globalization? Is globalization reinforcing nationalism or can it in some way be channelled in the opposite direction? What kind of nationalism is most likely to emerge with, or as a response to, globalization? Is globalization a causal factor in the explosion of ethnic conflict, xenophobia and racism?' (2002: 281).

Chapter 6. Justice: The Search for Solutions

1 In reality, the situation is much more complex than this. The Saudis, Turks and Egyptians are predominantly from the Sunni branches of Islam, while Iranians, Syrians, and many Lebanese Muslims and Iraqis, are largely Shiites. If you add Kurdish, Christian and Jewish communities, and in the latter case Israel, into the mix the true complexities of the societies start to emerge.

2 For an exploration of the politics of caste in India and how the 'untouchables' redefined themselves as *dalits*, see Anupama Rao (2009). It is another society faced with the central contradiction between a democratic political philosophy and flagrant discrimination against minority citizens.

3 While most of the traditional debate in India has focused on the disadvantages of those at the bottom of the caste hierarchy, more recently the situation of the very significant Muslim minority that has been totally outside the range of such redistributive policies has entered the discussion (Yardley 2012). In certain respects, this follows the experience of the United States where affirmative action policies have been extended to an ever-widening group of beneficiaries, including immigrants of colour and women. Some African Americans and Native Americans have objected strenuously to such measures, suggesting that they benefit groups who do not have a legitimate claim to such restitution.

4 In an article published in *Sociology* 34/3 (2000): 481–98, Michael Banton explores the notion of 'ethnic alignment', demonstrating when individuals, in the Malaysian case, decide to mobilize for collective action and when they do not. There are many examples in the United States where some minority individuals, often those holding strong conservative convictions, have become severe critics of affirmative action. The Stanford economist Thomas Sowell is one prominent example (Sowell 2004).

5 An increasingly cogent counter-attack against the critics of affirmative action, stresses the extent to which 'invisible' policies and programmes designed to assist the majority might equally be defined as 'affirmative action'. See Ira Katznelson, *When Affirmative Action was White* (2006), and Richard Kahlenberg, *Affirmative Action for the Rich* (2010). They demonstrate that the GI Bill promoting educational opportunities and house ownership for returning (white) veterans from the Second World War, as well as 'legacy preferences' for the children of alumni and wealthy donors at many prestigious American universities, are examples of preference policies for relatively advantaged groups in society. Such policies are rarely attacked by the opponents of affirmative action for deprived racial minorities. On the issue of 'effectiveness', the manner in which the apartheid policies in South Africa (1948–90) helped to transform poor whites (particularly Afrikaners) into well-educated and comfortable members of the white elite, in less than four decades, suggests that redistributive policies can be very successful!

6 It is true that some analysts examined the possibility of a peaceful transition in South Africa long before the actual process seemed more than a pipedream (Hanf et. al. 1981) and this literature began to accelerate towards the end of the 1980s (see Adam and Moodley 1986; Berger and Godsell (eds) 1988; Horowitz 1991).

7 Another interesting angle on explaining the reversal of situations of extreme polarization can be seen in the controversial ideas of the conflict-resolution specialist John Burton with his notion of basic human needs. See Avruch (2012: 126).

8 This position recognizes the objections raised by those social scientists concerned with what they see as 'collectivist' or 'essentialist' tendencies in much work in the field. How you can integrate the 'one and the many' when it comes to race, ethnicity and nationalism still remains a controversial issue. See the arguments of Michael Hechter (1987); Michael Banton (2007, 2014) and Rogers Brubaker (2004, 2013) on this issue. We are less than convinced by the 'solutions' these scholars employ to address this conundrum.

9 Elias during his time in England did attempt to address the obvious anomaly between an interpretation of social change based on increasing forms of 'civilized' behaviour and 'the breakdown of civilization' under National Socialism. While the 'rise of the fork' might be emblematic of important social changes, the development of the gas chamber suggests a rather different

aspect of European history. To be fair, Elias had published an insightful essay on 'The Expulsion of the Huguenots from France' that contained many insights into the vulnerability of economically successful, religious minorities in European societies in earlier times. The fact that this was occurring in the twentieth century, in this case involving Germany's Jewish community, raised a fundamental need to evaluate the precise meaning of the 'civilizing process' as applied in the European context (see Johan Goudsblom and Stephen Mennell (eds), *The Norbert Elias Reader* (Oxford: Blackwell, 1998).

10 Amartya Sen's conclusion concerning the relationship between violence and civil society is particularly relevant here: 'Fatalistic theorists of civilizational clash and the hurried advocates of economic reductionism spurn an examination of the cultural and social factors as well as the features of political economy that are all-important in understanding violence in the world today. These elements do not work in isolation, and we have to resist the tempting shortcuts that claim to deliver insight through single-minded concentration on one factor or another, ignoring other important features of an integrated picture. Perhaps most importantly, we have reason to understand that these distinct causal antecedents of violence are not immovable objects that are able to defy and overwhelm all human efforts to create a more peaceful social order' (Sen 2012: 35; 2009).

Bibliography

Abraham, Gary (1992) *Max Weber and the Jewish Question*. Urbana, IL: University of Illinois Press.

Adam, Heribert and Kogila Moodley (1986) *South Africa without Apartheid*: *Dismantling Racial Domination*. Berkeley, CA: University of California Press.

Adam, Kanya (2000) *The Colour of Business*: *Managing Diversity in South Africa*. Basel, Switzerland: P. Schlettwein Publishing.

Aguilera, Michael and Douglas Massey (2003) Social Capital and the Wages of Mexican Migrants: New Hypotheses and Tests. *Social Forces* 82: 671–701.

Alba, Richard (2005) Bright vs. Blurred Boundaries: Second-generation Assimilation and Exclusion in France, Germany, and the United States. *Ethnic and Racial Studies* 28: 20–49.

Alba, Richard (2009) *Blurring the Color Line*: *The New Chance for an Integrated America*. Cambridge, MA: Harvard University Press.

Alba, Richard, Peter Schmidt and Martina Wasmer (eds) (2003) *Germans or Foreigners?*: *Attitudes toward Ethnic Minorities in Post-Reunification Germany*. New York, NY: Palgrave Macmillan.

Alexander, Michelle (2010) *The New Jim Crow*: *Mass Incarceration in the Age of Colorblindness*. New York, NY: New Press.

Ancona, Deborah, Thomas Kochan, Maureen Scully, John van Maanen and Eleanor D. Westney (2005) *Managing for the Future*: *Organizational Behaviour and Processes* (3rd edn). Cincinnati, OH: South-Western College Publishing.

Anderson, Stacey (2013) Black People Still Face Inequality. *Associated Press*, 11 April.

Arendt, Hannah (1964) *Eichmann in Jerusalem*: *A Report on the Banality of Evil*. New York, NY: Penguin Books.

Avruch, Kevin (2003) Culture and Ethnic Conflict in the New World Disorder. In John Stone and Rutledge Dennis (eds), *Race and Ethnicity*: *Comparative and Theoretical Approaches*. Oxford: Blackwell, pp. 72–82.

Bibliography

Avruch, Kevin (2012) *Context and Pretext in Conflict Resolution: Identity, Power and Practice*. Boulder, CO: Paradigm Publishers.

Bacevich, Andrew (2008) *The Limits of Power: The End of American Exceptionalism*. New York, NY: Henry Holt.

Bailey, Stanley (2009) *Legacies of Race: Identities, Attitudes, and Politics in Brazil*. Stanford, CA: Stanford University Press.

Balakian, Peter (2003) *The Burning Tigris: The Armenian Genocide and America's Response*. New York: HarperCollins.

Banton, Michael (1983) *Racial and Ethnic Competition*. Cambridge: Cambridge University Press.

Banton, Michael (2000) Ethnic Conflict. *Sociology* 34: 481–98.

Banton, Michael (2002) *The International Politics of Race*. Cambridge: Polity.

Banton, Michael (2007) Max Weber on Ethnic Communities: A Critique. *Nations and Nationalism* 13: 19–35.

Banton, Michael (2013) In Defense of Mainstream Sociology. *Ethnic and Racial Studies* 36: 1000–4.

Banton, Michael (2014) Updating Max Weber on the Racial, the Ethnic, and the National. *Journal of Classical Sociology* 14/3. DOI: 10.1177/1468795X13494134; Online version at: <http://jcs.sagepub.com/content/early/2013/07/19/1468795X13494134>.

Barfield, Thomas (2010) *Afghanistan: A Cultural and Political History*. Princeton, NJ: Princeton University Press.

Barth, Fredrik (1969) *Ethnic Groups and Boundaries: The Social Organization of Cultural Difference*. Oslo: Universitetsforlaget.

Beechler, Schon and Ian C. Woodward (2009) The Global 'War for Talent'. *Journal of International Management* 15: 273–85.

Bellah, Robert (1957) *Tokugawa Religion: The Cultural Roots of Modern Japan*. Glencoe, IL: The Free Press.

Berger, Peter and Thomas Luckmann (1966) *The Social Construction of Reality: A Treatise in the Sociology of Knowledge*. Garden City, NY: Anchor Books.

Berger, Peter and Bobby Godsell (eds) (1988) *A Future South Africa: Visions, Strategies and Realities*. Boulder, CO: Westview Press.

Berger, Peter and Samuel Huntington (eds) (2002) *Many Globalizations: Cultural Diversity in the Contemporary World*. New York, NY: Oxford University Press.

Bloomberg News (2013) Immigrants Key to the Future, Merkel says. *Boston Globe*, 15 June.

Blumer, Herbert (1958) Race Prejudice as a Sense of Group Position. *Pacific Sociological Review* 1: 3–7.

Bobo, Lawrence (2011) Somewhere between Jim Crow and Post-Racialism: Reflections on the American Divide in America Today. *Daedalus* 140: 11–36.

Bonilla-Silva, Eduardo (1997) Rethinking Racism. *American Sociological Review* 62: 465–80.

Bonilla-Silva, Eduardo (2006) *Racism Without Racists: Colour-Blind Racism* and the Persistence of Racial Equality in the United States (2nd edn). Lanham, MD: Rowman and Littlefield.

Bonilla-Silva, Eduardo (2012) The Invisible Weight of Whiteness: The Racial Grammar of Everyday Life in Contemporary America. *Ethnic and Racial Studies* 35/2:173–94.

Brimelow, Peter (1995) *Alien Nation: Commonsense about America's Immigration Disaster*. New York, NY: Harper Perennial.

Brogan, Hugh (2006) *Alexis de Tocqueville: A Life*. New Haven, CT: Yale University Press.

Brubaker, Rogers (1992) *Citizenship and Nationhood in France and Germany*. Cambridge, MA: Harvard University Press.

Brubaker, Rogers (2004) *Ethnicity Without Groups*. Cambridge, MA: Harvard University Press.

Brubaker, Rogers (2013) Categories of Analysis and Categories of Practice: A Note on the Study of Muslims in European Countries of Immigration. *Ethnic and Racial Studies* 36: 1–8.

Bulmer, Martin and John Solomos (eds) (2010) *Muslim Minorities in Western Europe*. Themed Section, *Ethnic and Racial Studies* 33: 373–472.

Bureau of Labor Statistics, United States Department of Labor, The Editor's Desk, *Racial and Ethnic Characteristics of the U.S. Labor Force*, 2011. At: <http://www.bls.gov/opub/ted/2012/ted_20120905.htm>.

Campbell, Donald T. (1965) Ethnocentric and Other Altruistic Motives. In D. LeVine (ed.), *Nebraska Symposium on Motivation*. Lincoln, NE: University of Nebraska Press, pp. 283–311.

Canellos, Peter (2012) Can Censorship Help Heal Rwanda? *Boston Globe*, 5 February.

Casiro, Jessica (2006) Argentine Rescuers: A Study on the 'Banality of Good.' *Journal of Genocide Research* 8: 437–54.

Casiro, Jessica (2010) *Angels in Hell: Argentina's Willing Altruists?: A Study of Argentine Rescuers during the Political Killings of 1976–1983*. Saarbrucken, Germany: VDM Verlag.

Chambers, Elizabeth, Mark Foulon, Helen Hadfield-Jones, Steven Hankin and Edward Michaels III (1998) The War for Talent. *The McKinsey Quarterly* 3: 44–57.

Chase-Dunn, Christopher (1991) *Global Formation: Structures of the World Economy*. Oxford: Blackwell.

Chetty, Raj, Nathaniel Hendren, Patrick Kline, Emmanuel Saez and Nicholas Turner (2013) *The Equality of Opportunity Project*. At: <www.equality-of-opportunity.org>.

Clausewitz, Carl von (1984) [1832] *On War*, ed. Michael Howard and Peter Paret. Princeton NJ: Princeton University Press.

Chua, Vincent (2011) Social Networks and Labour Market Outcomes in a Meritocracy. *Social Networks* 33:1–11.

Bibliography

Cohen, Jon and Dan Balz (2013) Zimmerman Verdict Poll Finds Chasm between White and Black Reactions. *Washington Post* (22 July 2013). At: <http://www.washingtonpost.com/politics/race-shapes-zimmerman-verdict-re action/2013/07/22/3569662c-f2fc-11e2-8505-bf6f231e77b4_story.html>.

Connor, Walker (1984) *The National Question in Marxist-Leninist Theory and Strategy.* Princeton, NJ: Princeton University Press.

Connor, Walker (1994) *Ethnonationalism: The Quest for Understanding.* Princeton, NJ: Princeton University Press.

Conversi, Daniele (ed.) (2002) *Ethnonationalism in the Contemporary World: Walker Connor and the Study of Nationalism.* London: Routledge.

Conversi, Daniele (2004) Can Nationalism Studies and Ethnic and Racial Studies Be Brought Together? *Journal of Ethnic and Migration Studies* 30: 815–29.

Coser, Lewis (1956) *The Functions of Social Conflict.* New York, NY: The Free Press.

Coulter, Jeff and Wes Sharrock (2007) *Brain, Mind and Human Behaviour in Contemporary Cognitive Science,* New York, NY: Edwin Mellen Press.

Dennis, Rutledge (2003) W. E. B. Du Bois's Concept of Double Consciousness. In John Stone and Rutledge Dennis (eds), *Race and Ethnicity: Comparative and Theoretical Approaches.* Oxford: Blackwell, pp. 13–27.

Dennis, Rutledge (2013) Convergences and Divergences in Race Theorizing: A Critical Assessment of Race Formation Theory and Systemic Racism Theory. *Ethnic and Racial Studies* 36: 975-988.

Deshpande, Ashwini (2006) *Affirmative Action in India and the United States.* Washington DC: World Bank (World Development Report).

Dignan, Don (1981) Europe's Melting Pot: A Century of Large-scale Immigration into France. *Ethnic and Racial Studies* 4:137–52.

Dikötter, Frank (1997) The Construction of Racial Identities in China and Japan. Reprinted in John Stone and Rutledge Dennis (eds) (2003), *Race and Ethnicity: Comparative and Theoretical Approaches.* Oxford: Blackwell.

DiTomaso, Nancy (2013) *The American Non-Dilemma: Racial Inequality Without Racism.* New York, NY: Russell Sage Foundation.

Dreyer, June (1976) *China's Forty Millions: Minority Nationalities and National Integration in the People's Republic of China.* Cambridge, MA: Harvard University Press.

Du Bois, William E. B. (1903) *The Souls of Black Folk.* Chicago, IL: A.C. McClurg & Co.

Eastwood, Jonathan (2006) *The Rise of Nationalism in Venezuela.* Gainsville, FL: University Press of Florida.

Eastwood, Jonathan and John Stone (2007) Democracy Despite Despotism: A Latin American Paradox. *Theory and Society* 36: 111–16.

Eckstein, Susan (2009) *The Immigrant Divide: How Cuban Americans Changed the United States and Their Homeland.* New York, NY: Routledge.

Bibliography

The Economist (2006) *Survey: Talent.* The Economist, at: <http://www.econo mist.com>; 5 October.

Elliott, James R. (1999) Social Isolation and Labour Market Insulation: Network and Neighbourhood Effects on Less-Educated Urban Workers. *The Sociological Quarterly* 40:199–216.

Elliott, James R. (2001) Referral Hiring and Ethnically Homogeneous Jobs: How Prevalent is the Connection and for Whom? *Social Science Research* 30: 401–25.

Erickson, Bonnie H. (2001) Good Networks and Good Jobs: The Value of Social Capital to Employers and Employees. In Susan Cook, Nan Lin and Ronald Burt (eds), *Social Capital: Theory and Research.* New York: Aldine De Gruyter, pp. 127–58.

Falcon, Luis and Edwin Melendez (2001) The Social Context of Job Searching for Racial Groups in Urban Centers. In Alice O'Connor, Chris Tilly and Lawrence Bobo (eds), *Urban Inequality: Evidence from Four Cities.* New York: Russell Sage, pp. 341–71.

Feeney, Mark (2013) Nelson Mandela, a Lasting Force for Freedom, Dies. *Boston Globe,* 5 December.

Fernandez, Roberto and Isabel Fernandez-Mateo (2006) Networks, Race, and Hiring. *American Sociological Review* 71: 42–71.

Fernandez, Roberto, Emilio Castilla and Paul Moore (2000) Social Capital at Work: Networks and Employment at a Phone Centre. *American Journal of Sociology* 105: 1288–1356.

Fletcher, Michael A. (2013) College Students Take Racially Separate Paths, Study Says. *Washington Post,* 1 August. At: <http://www.bostonglobe.com/news/ nation/2013/07/31/report-says-minorities-and-whites-follow-unequal-college-paths/Zv2mGvupKKVMllkjKBbRvM/story.html>.

Foner, Nancy and Richard Alba (2010) Immigration and the Legacies of the Past: The Impact of Slavery and the Holocaust on Contemporary Immigrants in the United States and Western Europe. *Comparative Studies in Society and History* 52: 798–819.

Freyre, Gilberto (1933) [1986] *The Masters and the Slaves: A Study in the Development of Brazilian Civilization.* Berkeley, CA: University of California Press. (First published in Portuguese as *Casa-Grande & Senzala.*)

Fritz, Catarina (2011) *Brazilian Immigrants and the Quest for Identity.* El Paso, TX: LFB Scholarly Publishing.

Fritz, Catarina and John Stone (2009) A Post-racial America: Myth or Reality? *Ethnic and Racial Studies* 32: 1083–9.

Furnivall, John Sydenham (1939) *Netherlands India: A Study of Plural Economy.* Cambridge: Cambridge University Press.

Furnivall, John Sydenham (1948) *Colonial Policy and Practice.* Cambridge: Cambridge University Press.

Gerhards, Jurgen and Silke Hans (2011) Why Not Turkey? Attitudes towards

Bibliography

Turkish Membership in the EU. *Journal of Common Market Studies* 49: 741–66.

Giddens, Anthony (1971) *Capitalism and Modern Social Theory.* Cambridge: Cambridge University Press.

Giddens, Anthony (1981) *A Contemporary Critique of Historical Materialism.* London: Macmillan.

Glaeser, Edward and Jacob Vigdor (2012) *The End of the Segregated Century: Racial Separation in America's Neighborhoods, 1890–2010.* Manhattan Institute: Civic Report 66 (January).

Go, Julian (2008) *American Empire and the Politics of Meaning.* Durham, NC, and London: Duke University Press.

Go, Julian (2011) *Patterns of Empire: The British and American Empires, 1688 to the Present.* New York, NY: Cambridge University Press.

Gobineau, Arthur de [1853–5] (1915) [An Essay on] *The Inequality of the Human Races.* New York: G.P. Putnam's Sons.

Gordon, Milton (1964) *Assimilation in American Life: The Role of Race, Religion and National Origins.* New York, NY: Oxford University Press.

Goudsblom, Johan and Stephen Mennell (eds) (1998) *The Norbert Elias Reader.* Oxford: Blackwell.

Granovetter, Mark (1973) The Strength of Weak Ties. *American Journal of Sociology* 78: 1360–80.

Granovetter, Mark (1995) [1974] *Getting a Job.* Chicago, IL: University of Chicago Press.

Green, Gary, Leann Tigges and Daniel Diaz (1999) Racial and Ethnic Differences in Job-Search Strategies in Atlanta, Boston, and Los Angeles. *Social Science Quarterly* 80: 263–78.

Hanf, Theodor, Heribert Weiland and Gerda Vierdag (1981) *South Africa: The Prospects of Peaceful Change.* London: Rex Collings.

Hartz, Louis (1955) *The Liberal Tradition in America.* New York, NY: Harcourt Brace.

Hechter, Michael (1975) *Internal Colonialism: The Celtic Fringe in British National Development.* London: Routledge.

Hechter, Michael (1986) Rational Choice and the Study of Race and Ethnic Relations. In John Rex and D. Mason (eds), *Theories of Race and Ethnic Relations.* Cambridge: Cambridge University Press, pp. 264–79.

Hechter, Michael (1987) *Principles of Group Solidarity.* Berkeley, CA: University of California Press.

Herman, Melissa and Mary Campbell (2012) 'I Wouldn't but You Can': Attitudes Toward Interracial Relationships. *Social Science Research* 41: 343–58.

Hochschild, Adam (1998) *King Leopold's Ghost: A Story of Greed, Terror, and Heroism in Colonial Africa.* New York, NY: Houghton Mifflin.

Hochschild, Jennifer and Vesla Weaver (2007) The Skin Colour Paradox and the American Racial Order. *Social Forces* 86: 643–70.

Bibliography

Hockstader, Lee (2010) Even as Population Shrinks, Japan Remains Wary of Immigration. *Washington Post*, 14 March.

Holzer, Harry, Joleen Kirschenman, Philip Moss and Chris Tilly (2000) Multi-City Study of Urban Inequality, 1992–1994: Atlanta, Boston, and Los Angeles. *Social Science Quarterly* 80: 263–78.

Horowitz, Donald (1971) Three Dimensions of Ethnic Politics. *World Politics* 23: 232–44.

Horowitz, Donald (1985) *Ethnic Groups in Conflict*. Berkeley, CA: University of California Press.

Horowitz, Donald (1991) *A Democratic South Africa? Constitutional Engineering in a Divided Society*. Berkeley, CA: University of California Press.

Hou, Xiaoshuo (2011) From Mao to the Market: Community Capitalism in Rural China. *Theory, Culture and Society* 28: 46–68.

Hou, Xiaoshuo (2013) *Community Capitalism in China: The State, the Market, and Collectivism*. New York: Cambridge University Press.

Hou, Xiaoshuo and John Stone (2008) The Ethnic Dilemma in China's Industrial Revolution. *Ethnic and Racial Studies* 31: 812–17.

Huntington, Samuel (1996) *The Clash of Civilizations and the Remaking of World Order*. New York, NY: Simon and Schuster.

Huntington, Samuel (2004) *Who Are We?: The Challenges to America's National Identity*. New York, NY: Simon and Schuster.

Hutchinson, John (2005) *Nations as Zones of Conflict*. London: Sage Publications.

Iles, Paul, Abdoul Almhedie and Baruch Yehuda (2012) Managing HR in the Middle East: Challenges in the Public Sector. *Public Personnel Management* 41: 465–92.

Jain, Sonali (2011) The Rights of 'Return': Ethnic Identities in the Workplace among Second Generation Indian American Professionals in the Parental Homeland. *Journal of Ethnic and Migration Studies* 37:1313–30.

Jain, Sonali (2013) For Love and Money: Second-Generation Indian-Americans 'Return' to India. *Ethnic and Racial Studies* 36: 896–914.

Joas, Hans (1999) The Modernity of War: Modernization Theory and the Problem of Violence. *International Sociology* 14/4 (December): 457–72.

Johnson, Bradford C., James M. Manyika and Lareina A. Yee (2005) The Next Revolution in Interactions. *McKinsey Quarterly* 4: 20–33.

Jolly, Seth and Sibel Oktay (2012) Rising Euroskepticism: Evolving Turkish Attitudes Towards the EU. Syracuse University. Paper delivered to Midwest Political Science Association.

Kahlenberg, Richard D. (2010) *Affirmative Action for the Rich: Legacy Preferences in College Admissions*. New York, NY: The Century Foundation Press.

Kaltman, Blaine (2007) *Under the Heel of the Dragon: Islam, Racism, Crime and the Uighur in China*. Athens, OH: Ohio University Press.

Bibliography

Katz, Fred E. (1993) *Ordinary People and Extraordinary Evil: A Report on the Beguilings of Evil.* Albany, NY: SUNY Press.

Katz, Fred E. (2004) *Confronting Evil: Two Journeys.* Albany, NY: SUNY Press.

Katznelson, Ira (2006) *When Affirmative Action was White: An Untold History of Racial Inequality in the Twentieth Century.* New York, NY: Norton.

Keevak, Michael (2011) *Becoming Yellow: A Short History of Racial Thinking.* Princeton, NJ: Princeton University Press.

Kennedy, John F. (1964) *A Nation of Immigrants.* New York: Harper and Row.

Kibria, Nazli (2011) *Muslims in Motion: Islam and National Identity in the Bangladeshi Diaspora.* New Brunswick, NJ: Rutgers University Press.

Kirk-Greene, Anthony (ed.) (1979) *The Transfer of Power in Africa: The Colonial Administrator in the Age of De-colonization.* Oxford: Oxford University Press African Studies Series.

Kmec, Julie A. and Lindsey B. Trimble (2009) Does it Pay to Have a Network Contact? Social Network Ties, Workplace Racial Context, and Pay Outcomes. *Social Science Research* 38: 266–78.

Kozol, Jonathan (2005) *The Shame of the Nation: The Restoration of Apartheid Schooling in America.* New York: Crown Publishers.

Kuhn, Thomas (1962) *The Structure of Scientific Revolutions.* Chicago, IL: Chicago University Press.

Kuper, Leo (1983) *Genocide: Its Political Use in the Twentieth Century.* New Haven, CT: Yale University Press.

Kuper, Leo (1985) *The Prevention of Genocide.* New Haven, CT: Yale University Press.

Kuper, Leo and M. G. Smith (eds) (1969) *Pluralism in Africa.* Berkeley, CA: University of California Press.

Lake, David A. and Donald Rothchild (1996) Containing Fear: The Origins and Management of Ethnic Conflict. *International Security* 21: 41–75.

Lal, Barbara (1990) *The Romance of Culture in an Urban Civilization: Robert E. Park on Race and Ethnic Relations in Cities.* London: Routledge.

Lamont, Michèle and Nissim Mizrachi (eds) (2012) Ordinary People Doing Extraordinary Things: Responses to Stigmatization in Comparative Perspective: Brazil, Canada, Israel, France, South Africa, Sweden and the United States. *Ethnic and Racial Studies* 35/3: 365–81.

Lazarova, Mila and Sully Taylor (2009) Boundaryless Career, Social Capital, and Knowledge Management: Implications for Performance. *Journal of Organizational Behaviour* 30: 119–39.

Lee, Jennifer and Frank Bean (2010) *The Diversity Paradox: Immigration and the Color Line in Twenty-First Century America.* New York, NY: Russell Sage Foundation.

Lemarchand, Rene (1994) *Burundi: Ethnic Conflict and Genocide.* Cambridge: Woodrow Wilson Centre Press and Cambridge University Press.

Leoussi, Athena and Steven Grosby (eds) (2007) *Nationalism and Ethnosymbolism:*

History, Culture and Ethnicity in the Formation of Nations. Edinburgh: Edinburgh University Press.

Levin, Michael and John Stone (1985) Nationalism, Racism and the 'Marxist Question'. In *Marxist Perspectives on Ethnicity and Nationalism*. Belgrade: Institute of Political Studies, pp. 1–23.

LeVine, Robert A. and Donald T. Campbell (1972) *Ethnocentrism: Theories of Conflict, Ethnic Attitudes, and Group Behaviour*. New York: Wiley.

Levitt, Peggy and Mary Waters (eds) (2002) *The Changing Face of Home: The Transnational Lives of the Second Generation*. New York, NY: Russell Sage Foundation.

Lie, John (2001) *Multi-Ethnic Japan*. Cambridge, MA: Harvard University Press.

Lim, Mah Hui (1985) Affirmative Action, Ethnicity and Integration: The Case of Malaysia. *Ethnic and Racial Studies* 8: 250–76.

Lin, Nan (1999) Social Networks and Status Attainment. *Annual Review of Sociology* 25: 467–87.

Lin, Nan (2009) Production and Returns of Social Capital – Evidence from Urban China. In Ray-May Hsung, Nan Lin and Ronald L. Breiger (eds), *Contexts of Social Capital – Social Networks in Markets, Communities, and Families*. New York, NY: Routledge, pp. 163–92.

Lin, Nan, Zhang Yanlong, Chen Wenhong, Dan Ao and Song Lijun (2009) Recruiting and Deploying Social Capital in Organizations: Theory and Evidence. In Lisa Keister (ed.), *Work and Organizations in China After Thirty Years of Transition* (Research in the Sociology of Work (19)). Bingley: Emerald Group Publishing Limited, pp. 225–51.

Lipka, Sara (2013) Fisher versus the University of Texas. *Chronicle of Higher Education*, 5 July.

Lipset, Seymour M. (1963) *The First New Nation: The United States in Historical and Comparative Perspective*. New York, NY: Basic Books.

Lipset, Seymour M. (1996) *American Exceptionalism: A Double-Edged Sword*. New York, NY: Norton.

Longman, Timothy (2011) *Christianity and Genocide in Rwanda*. Cambridge: Cambridge University Press.

Loury, Glenn, Tariq Modood and Stephen Telles (eds) (2005) *Ethnicity, Social Mobility and Public Policy: Comparing the US and UK*. Cambridge: Cambridge University Press.

Loveman, Mara, Jeronimo Muniz and Stanley Bailey (2012) Brazil in Black and White? Race Categories, the Census, and the Study of Inequality. *Ethnic and Racial Studies* 35: 1466–83.

Lowenheim, Oded (2006) *Predators and Parasites: Persistent Agents of Transnational Harm and Great Power Authority*. Ann Arbor, MI: University of Michigan Press.

Lowrey, Annie (2013) Wealth Gap Between Whites, Minorities Widening. *New York Times*, 29 April.

Bibliography

Lukacs, John (ed.) (1968) *Alexis de Tocqueville: The European Revolution and Correspondence with Gobineau.* Gloucester, MA: Peter Smith.

Lukes, Steven (2005) [1974] *Power: A Radical View* (2nd edn). London: Palgrave Macmillan.

McDonald, Steve, Nan Lin and Dan Ao (2009) Networks of Opportunity: Gender, Race, and Job Leads. *Social Problems* 56: 385–402.

McKernan, Signe-Mary, Caroline Ratcliffe, C. Eugene Steuer and Sisi Zhang (2013) Urban Institute Report, *Less than Equal: Racial Disparities in Wealth Accumulation* (26 April). At: <http://www.urban.org/UploadedPDF/412802-Less-Than-Equal-Racial-Disparities-in-Wealth-Accumulation.pdf>.

Maleki, Edward J. and Michael C. Ewers (2007) Labour Migration to World Cities with a Research Agenda for the Arab Gulf. *Progress in Human Geography* 31: 467–84.

Manasse, Ernst (1947) Max Weber on Race. *Social Research* 14: 191–221.

Mann, Michael (2005) *The Dark Side of Democracy: Explaining Ethnic Cleansing.* Cambridge: Cambridge University Press.

Manz, Charles, Frank Shipper and Greg Stewart (2009) Everyone a Team Leader: Shared Influence at W.L. Gore & Associates. *Organizational Dynamics* 38: 239–44.

Manza, Jeff (1992) Classes, Status Groups and Social Closure: A Critique of Neo-Weberian Social Theory. *Current Perspectives in Social Theory* 12: 275–302.

Martin, Eric (2012) Move Over, BRIC Nations: Investors Have Discovered MIST. *Boston Globe*, 14 August.

Martineau, Harriet (1981) [1837] *Society in America.* (ed. S. M. Lipset). New Brunswick, NJ: Transaction Publishers.

Marx, Anthony (1998) *Making Race and Nation: A Comparison of the United States, South Africa and Brazil.* Cambridge: Cambridge University Press.

Mason, Philip (1970) *Patterns of Dominance.* London: Oxford University Press.

Massey, Douglas (2007) *Categorically Unequal.* New York, NY: Russell Sage.

Massey, Douglas and Nancy Denton (1993) *American Apartheid: Segregation and the Making of the Underclass.* Cambridge, MA: Harvard University Press.

Mennell, Stephen. J. (1969) Prohibition: A Sociological View. *Journal of American Studies* 3/1 (December): 159–75.

Merton, Robert (1949) Discrimination and the American Creed. In R. M. MacIver (ed.), *Discrimination and National Welfare.* New York, NY: Harper, pp. 77–145.

Merton, Robert (1995) The Thomas Theorem and the Matthew Effect. *Social Forces* 74: 379–424.

Mintz, Beth, and Daniel Krymkowski (2010) The Ethnic, Race, and Gender Gaps on Workplace Authority: Changes over Time in the United States. *The Sociological Quarterly* 51: 20–45.

Mitchell, Lawrence (2001) *Corporate Irresponsibility: America's Newest Export.* New Haven, CT: Yale University Press.

Bibliography

Moskos, Charles and John S. Butler (1996) *All That We Can Be: Black Leadership and Racial Integration the Army Way*. New York: Basic Books.

Mouw, Ted (2002) Are Black Workers Missing the Connection? The Effect of Spatial Distance and Employee Referrals on Inter-firm Racial Segregation. *Demography* 39: 507–28.

Mouw, Ted (2003) Social Capital and Finding a Job: Do Contacts Matter? *American Sociological Review* 68 (December): 868–98.

Murphy, Raymond (1988) *Social Closure: The Theory of Monopolization and Exclusion*. New York, NY: Oxford University Press.

Naithani, Pranav and A. N. Jha, (2010) Challenges Faced by Expatriate Workers in Gulf Cooperation Council Countries. *International Journal of Business and Management* 5: 98–103.

National Urban League (2013) *The State of Black America, Redeem the Dream: Jobs Rebuild America*. At: <http://iamempowered.com/node/74570>.

Nightingale, Carl (2012) *Segregation: A Global History of Divided Cities*. Chicago, IL: University of Chicago Press.

Nishida, Masayo (2008) *Migrants of Choice: Contemporary German and Japanese Professionals Living in the United States*. PhD Dissertation, Boston University.

Nye, Joseph (2003) *The Paradox of American Power: Why the World's Only Superpower Can't Go it Alone*. New York, NY: Oxford University Press.

Nye, Joseph (2004) *Soft Power: The Means to Success in World Politics*. New York, NY: Public Affairs.

Nye, Joseph (2011) *The Future of Power*. New York, NY: Public Affairs.

O'Dowd, Amie (2005) Establishing Boundaries: A Comparative Analysis of Immigrants as Outsiders in Ireland and Italy, unpublished PhD thesis, University College, Dublin.

OECD (2006) Good Governance for Development in Arab Countries Initiative. At: <www.oecd.org/countries/unitedarabemirates/37208619.pdf>.

Okamura, Jonathan (1981) Situational Ethnicity. *Ethnic and Racial Studies* 4: 452–65.

Omi, Michael and Howard Winant (2013) Resistance is Futile? A Response to Feagin and Elias. *Ethnic and Racial Studies* 36: 961–73.

Parekh, Bhikhu (1997) *Gandhi*. Oxford: Oxford University Press.

Pareto, Vilfredo (1902) *Les Systèmes Socialistes*. Paris: V. Giard and E. Brière.

Park, Robert E. (1928) Human Migration and the Marginal Man. *The American Journal of Sociology* 33/6: 881–93.

Park, Robert E. (1950) [1928] *Race and Culture*: Glencoe, IL: The Free Press.

Parkin, Frank (1979) *Marxism and Class Theory: A Bourgeois Critique*. New York, NY: Columbia University Press.

Parkin, Frank (1982) *Max Weber*. London: Tavistock Publications.

Pascale, Joassart-Marcelli and Philip Stephens (2010) Immigrant Banking and

Financial Exclusion in Greater Boston. *Journal of Economic Geography* 10: 883–912.

Passel, Jeffrey and Roberto Suro (2005) *Rise, Peak and Decline: Trends in US Immigration 1992–2004.* Washington DC: Pew Hispanic Centre Report.

Peel, John D. Y. (1971) *Herbert Spencer: The Evolution of a Sociologist.* London: Heinemann.

Petersen, Trond, Ishak Saporta and Marc-David L. Seidel (2000) Offering a Job: Meritocracy and Social Networks. *American Journal of Sociology* 106: 736–816.

Pew Research Center (2008) *The State of Marriage and Divorce (2008)* from the American Community Service, 15 October.

Pew Research Center Publications (2009) *Mapping the Global Muslim Population: A Report on the Size and Distribution of the World's Muslim Population* on-line, pewforum.org.

Pinker, Steven (2011) *The Better Angels of Our Nature: Why Violence Has Declined.* London: Penguin.

Portes, Alejandro (1995) Economic Sociology and the Sociology of Immigration: A Conceptual Overview. In A. Portes (ed.), *Economic Sociology of Immigration: Essays on Networks, Ethnicity and Entrepreneurship.* New York, NY: Russell Sage Foundation, pp. 1–41.

Portes, Alejandro and Alex Stepick (1993) *City on the Edge: The Transformation of Miami.* Berkeley, CA: University of California Press.

Portes, Alejandro and Ruben Rumbaut (2006) *Immigrant America: A Portrait.* Berkeley, CA: University of California Press.

PriceWaterhouseCoopers (2008). The 11th Annual Global CEO Survey: Competing and Collaborating. What is Success in a Connected World? Executive summary. At: <http://pwc.blogs.com/files/ceo-global-survey---exec-summary---18883_ceo3_exec_summary_v6.pdf>.

PriceWaterhouseCoopers (2014). The 17th Annual Global CEO Survey: Fit for the Future – Capitalizing on Global Trends. At: <http://www.pwc.com/gx/en/ceo-survey/2014/assets/pwc-17th-annual-global-ceo-survey-jan-2014.pdf>.

Prunier, Gerard (1995) *The Rwanda Crisis: History of a Genocide.* London: Hurst.

Prunier, Gerard (2005) *Darfur: The Ambiguous Genocide.* Ithaca, NY: Cornell University Press.

Rao, Anupama (2009) *The Caste Question: Dalits and the Politics of Modern India.* Berkeley and Los Angeles, CA: University of California Press.

Rex, John (1970) *Race Relations in Sociological Theory.* London: Weidenfeld and Nicolson.

Rex, John. (1980) The Theory of Race Relations: A Weberian Approach. In M. O'Callaghan (ed.), *Sociological Theories: Race and Colonialism.* Paris: UNESCO, pp. 117–42.

Richmond, Anthony (2003) Postindustrialism, Postmodernism, and Ethnic

Bibliography

Conflict. In John Stone and Rutledge Dennis (eds), *Race and Ethnicity: Comparative and Theoretical Approaches*. Oxford: Blackwell, pp. 83–94.

Rizova, Polly (2006) Balkanization. In George Ritzer (ed.), *The Blackwell Encyclopedia of Sociology*. New York, NY: Wiley-Blackwell, pp. 239–40.

Rizova, Polly (2007) *The Secret of Success: The Double Helix of Formal and Informal Structures in an R&D Laboratory*. Stanford, CA: Stanford University Press.

Roberts, Sam (2012) Segregation Curtailed in US Cities, Study Finds. *New York Times*, 31 January, A13.

Rogers, Ibram H. (2012) Brazil's Affirmative-Action Quotas: Progress? *The Chronicle of Higher Education*, 5 November.

Roth, Guenther and Claus Wittich (trans.) (1968) *Max Weber, Economy and Society: An Outline of Interpretive Sociology*. Berkeley, CA: University of California Press.

Roxborough, Ian (1999) The Persistence of War as a Sociological Problem. *International Sociology* 14/4: 491–500.

Roy, Beth (2003) Rioting Across Continental Divides. In John Stone and Rutledge Dennis (eds), *Race and Ethnicity: Comparative and Theoretical Approaches*. Oxford: Blackwell, pp. 191–207.

Royster, Deirdre A. (2003) *Race and the Invisible Hand: How White Networks Exclude Black Men From Blue Collar Jobs*. Berkeley and Los Angeles, CA: University of California Press.

Runciman, W. G. (ed.) (1978) *Max Weber: Selections in Translation*. Cambridge: Cambridge University Press.

Sambidge, Andy (2009) *Brit Expats Earn Double That of Indian Counterparts*. At: <http://www.arabianbusiness.com/brit-expats-earn-double-that-of-indian-counterparts-79468.html>.

Sanders, Jimy M. and Victor Nee (1996) Limits of Ethnic Solidarity in the Enclave Economy. *American Sociological Review* 61: 231–49.

Schama, Simon (2006) *Rough Crossings: Britain, the Slaves and the American Revolution*. New York, NY: Ecco Press.

Scheffer, Paul (2010) *The Open Society and Its Migrants* NECE paper at the Cities and Urban Spaces. European Conference, Trieste, Italy, (29 September–1 October 2010).

Scheffer, Paul (2011) *Immigrant Nations*. Cambridge: Polity.

Schmidt, Peter (2007) *Color or Money: How Rich White Kids Are Winning the War over College Affirmative Action*. New York, NY: Palgrave Macmillan.

Seidel, Marc-David L., Jeffrey T. Polzer and Katherine J. Stewart (2000) Friends in High Places: The Effects of Social Networks on Discrimination in Salary Negotiations. *Administrative Science Quarterly* 45: 1–24.

Sekulić, Duško (1997) The Creation and Dissolution of the Multinational State: The Case of Yugoslavia. *Nations and Nationalism* 3: 165–79.

Sekulić, Duško, Garth Massey and Randy Hodson (1994) Who Were the

Yugoslavs? Failed Sources of Identity in the Former Yugoslavia. *American Sociological Review* 59: 83–97.

Sekulić, Duško, Garth Massey and Randy Hodson (2006) Ethnic Intolerance and Ethnic Conflict in the Dissolution of Yugoslavia. *Ethnic and Racial Studies* 29: 797–827.

Semler, Ricardo (1993) *Maverick: The Success Story Behind the World's Most Unusual Workplace.* New York and Boston: Business Plus Press.

Sen, Amartya (2009) *The Idea of Justice.* Cambridge, MA: Harvard University Press.

Sen, Amartya (2012) Violence and Civil Society. *Cambridge Alumni Magazine* 64: 30–5.

Shapiro, Thomas (2004) *The Hidden Costs of Being African American.* New York, NY: Oxford University Press.

Sheth, Dhirubhai (1997) quoted in Kenneth Cooper, Classes Clash Over Quotas in India. *Washington Post*, 18 July. At: <http://www.hindunet.org/hvk/articles/0897/0100.html>.

Sidanius, Jim and Felicia Pratto (1999) *Social Dominance: An Intergroup Theory of Social Hierarchy and Oppression.* Cambridge: Cambridge University Press.

Simmel, Georg (1908) *Conflict.* In Kurt Wolff (trans.) *The Sociology of Georg Simmel.* Glencoe, IL: The Free Press (1950), pp. 13–17.

Skocpol, Theda and Vanessa Williamson (2012) *The Tea Party and the Remaking of Republican Conservatism.* New York, NY: Oxford University Press.

Smith, Anthony (1992) Chosen Peoples: Why Ethnic Groups Survive. *Ethnic and Racial Studies* 15: 436–56.

Smith, Anthony (1992b) Nationalism and the Historians. *International Journal of Comparative Sociology* 33: 58–80.

Smith, Anthony (2003) *Chosen Peoples: Sacred Sources of National Identity.* Oxford: Oxford University Press.

Smith, Anthony (2004) *The Antiquity of Nations.* Cambridge: Polity.

Smith, Peter B., Hai Juan Huang, Charles Harb, and Claudio Torres (2012) How Distinctive Are Indigenous Ways of Achieving Influence? A Comparative Study of Guanxi, Wasta, Jeitinho, and 'Pulling Strings'. *Journal of Cross-Cultural Psychology* 43: 135–50.

Smith, Sandra S. (2000). Mobilizing Social Resources: Race, Ethnic, and Gender Differences in Social Capital and Persisting Wage Inequalities. *The Sociological Quarterly* 41: 509–37.

Sowell, Thomas (2004) *Affirmative Action around the World: An Empirical Study.* New Haven, CT: Yale University Press.

Stainback, Kevin (2008) Social Contacts and Race/Ethnic Job Matching. *Social Forces* 87: 854–86.

Statistical Yearbook for Asia and the Pacific (2008) United Nations Economic and Social Commission for Asia and the Pacific. At: <http://www.unescap.org/stat/data/syb2008/escap-syb2008.pdf>.

Bibliography

Steinberg, Stephen (2007) *Race Relations: A Critique*. Stanford, CA: Stanford University Press.

Stephenson, Elizabeth and Adarsh Pandit (2008) How Companies Act on Global Trends: A McKinsey Global Survey. *The McKinsey Quarterly* (March): 2–9.

Stone, John (1973) *Colonist or Uitlander?* Oxford: Clarendon Press.

Stone, John (1977) *Race, Ethnicity, and Social Change*. Belmont, CA: Wadsworth.

Stone, John (1985) *Racial Conflict in Contemporary Society*. Cambridge, MA: Harvard University Press.

Stone, John (2002) Ethnonationalism in Black and White: Scholars and the South African Revolution. In Daniele Conversi (ed.), *Ethnonationalism in the Contemporary World: Walker Connor and the Study of Nationalism*. London: Routledge, pp. 113–29.

Stone, John (2004) Deconstructing Rational Choice: Or Why We Shouldn't Over-Rationalize the Non-Rational. *Journal of Ethnic and Migration Studies* 30: 841–3.

Stone, John and Stephen Mennell (1980) *Alexis de Tocqueville on Democracy, Revolution and Society*. Chicago, IL: Chicago University Press.

Stone, John and Polly Rizova (2007) Re-thinking Racial Conflict in an Era of Global Terror. *Ethnic and Racial Studies* 30: 534–45.

Stone, John and Rutledge Dennis (eds) (2003) *Race and Ethnicity: Comparative and Theoretical Approaches*. Oxford: Blackwell.

Stone, John and Michael Hechter (eds) (1979) *Internal Colonialism*: Special Issue of *Ethnic and Racial Studies* 2/3 (July): 255–399.

Stonequist, Everett (1937) *The Marginal Man: A Study in Personality and Culture*. New York: Charles Scribner's Sons.

Straus, Scott (2006) *The Order of Genocide: Race, Power and War in Rwanda*. Ithaca, NY: Cornell University Press.

Strohl, Jeff and Anthony Carnevale (2013) *Failure to Launch: Structural Shift and the New Lost Generation*. Center on Education and the Workforce Report, Washington DC: Georgetown University, 13 August. At: <www.cew. georgetown.edu/failuretolaunch>.

Svensson, Frances (1978) The Final Crisis of Tribalism: Comparative Ethnic Policy on American and Russian Frontiers. *Ethnic and Racial Studies* 1: 100–23.

Swartz, David (2007) Recasting Power in its Third Dimension. *Theory and Society* 36: 103–9.

Taylor, Marylee C. (1998) How White Attitudes Vary With the Racial Composition of Local Populations: Numbers Count. *American Sociological Review* 63: 512–35.

Telles, Edward (2004) *Race in Another America: The Significance of Skin Colour in Brazil*. Princeton, NJ: Princeton University Press.

Thomas, W. I. and Dorothy Thomas (1928) *The Child in America: Behavior Problems and Programs*. New York, NY: Knopf.

Bibliography

Tilly, Charles (1998) *Durable Inequality*, Berkeley, CA: University of California Press.

Tiryakian, Edward (1999) War: The Covered Side of Modernity. *International Sociology* 14: 4: 473–89.

Tocqueville, Alexis de [1835–40] (1956) *Democracy in America* (ed. Richard Heffner). New York, NY: Mentor Books.

Tocqueville, Alexis de [1856] (1966) *The Ancien Régime and the Revolution*. London: Fontana.

Tomaskovic-Devey, Donald (1993) *Gender and Racial Inequality at Work: The Sources and Consequences of Job Segregation*. Ithaca, NY: ILR/ Cornell University.

Tomaskovic-Devey, Donald and Kevin Stainback (2006) Discrimination and Desegregation: Equal Opportunity Progress in U.S. Private Sector Workplaces Since the Civil Rights Act. *Annals, AAPSS* 605: 1–36.

Tung, Rosalie L. and Lazarova, Mila (2006) Brain Drain versus Brain Gain: An Exploratory Study of Ex-Host Country Nationals in Central and East Europe. *International Journal of Human Resource Management* 17: 1853–72.

Vallas, Steven (2003) Rediscovering the Color Line within Work Organizations. *Work and Occupations* 30: 379–400.

Vallas, Steven (2012) *Work: A Critique*. Cambridge: Polity.

van Amersfoort, Hans (1996) Migration: The Limits of Government Control. *New Community* 22: 243–57.

van den Berghe, Pierre (1967) *South Africa: A Study in Conflict*. Middletown, CT: Wesleyan University Press.

van den Berghe, Pierre (1978) *Race and Racism: A Comparative Perspective*. New York, NY: John Wiley.

Vogel, Ezra (2011) *Deng Xiaoping and the Transformation of China*. Cambridge, MA: Belknap Press of Harvard University Press.

Wacquant, Loïc (2009) *Punishing the Poor: The Neoliberal Government of Social Insecurity*. Durham, NC: Duke University Press.

Wacquant, Loïc (2010) Class, Race and Hyperincarceration in Revanchist America. *Daedalus* (summer) 139: 3: 74–90.

Waldinger, Roger (1986) *Through the Eyes of the Needle: Immigrants and Enterprise in New York's Garment Trades*. New York, NY: New York University Press.

Waldron, Jeremy (2012) *The Harm in Hate Speech*. Cambridge, MA: Harvard University Press.

Wallerstein, Immanuel (1974) *The Modern World System 1: Capitalist Agriculture and the Origins of the European World Economy in the Sixteenth Century*. New York: Academic Press.

Wallman, Sandra (1986) Ethnicity and the Boundary Process in Context. In John Rex and David Mason (eds), *Theories of Race and Ethnic Relations*. Cambridge: Cambridge University Press, pp. 226–45.

Bibliography

Weber, Max (1904–5) *The Protestant Ethic and the Spirit of Capitalism*. New York, NY: Scribner.

Weber, Max (1922) *Economy and Society* (trans. and ed. G. Roth and C. Wittich (1968)). New York, NY: Bedminster.

Weitz, Eric (2003) *A Century of Genocide: Utopias of Race and Nation*. Princeton, NJ: Princeton University Press.

Williams, Katherine Y. and Charles A. O'Reilly (1998) Demography and Diversity in Organizations: A Review of 40 Years of Research. In B. M. Shaw and L. L. Cummings (eds), *Research in Organizational Behaviour*. Greenwich, CT: JAI Press, vol. 20, pp. 77–140.

Wilson, William J. (1987) *The Truly Disadvantaged: The Inner City, the Underclass, and Public Policy*. Chicago, IL: Chicago University Press.

Wilson, William J. (1996) *When Work Disappears: The World of the New Urban Poor*. New York, NY: Knopf.

Wilson, William J. (2009) *More Than Just Race: Being Black and Poor in the Inner City*. New York, NY: W.W. Norton.

Wimmer, Andreas (2011) A Swiss Anomaly? A Relational Account of National Boundary Making. *Nations and Nationalism* 17: 718–37.

Winant, Howard (2006) Race and Racism: Towards a Global Future. *Ethnic and Racial Studies* 29: 986–1003.

Wolff, Kurt (ed.) (1950) *The Sociology of Georg Simmel*. New York, NY: The Free Press.

Woodward, C. Vann (1951) *Origins of the New South, 1877–1913*. Baton Rouge, LA: Louisiana State University Press.

Woodward, C. Vann (1955) *The Strange Career of Jim Crow*. New York, NY: Oxford University Press.

Woolls, Daniel (2005) Six Africans Killed Near Spanish Enclave. *Boston Globe*, Friday 7 October.

Wrong, Dennis (1979) *Power: Its Forms, Bases and Uses*. Oxford: Blackwell.

Yanjie Bian, Xianbi Huang. 2009. *Network Resources and Job Mobility in China's Transitional Economy*. In Lisa Keister (ed.), *Work and Organizations in China After Thirty Years of Transition (Research in the Sociology of Work, Volume 19)*. Bingley: Emerald Group Publishing Limited, pp. 255–82.

Yardley, Jim (2012) India Eyes Muslims left behind by Quota System. *New York Times*, 9 March.

Zang, Xiaowei (2007) *Ethnicity and Urban Life in China: A Comparative Study of Hui Muslims and Han Chinese*. New York: Routledge.

Zhu, Yuchao and Dongyan Blachford (2012) Economic Expansion, Marketization, and Their Social Impact on China's Ethnic Minorities in Xinjiang and Tibet. *Asian Survey* 52: 714–33.

Zolberg, Aristide and Long Woon (1999) Why Islam is like Spanish: Cultural Incorporation in Europe and the United States. *Politics and Society* 27: 5–38.

Index

Index

Index

Index

Index